Now That
YOU'RE
SOBER

Now That
YOU'RE
SOBER

Week-by-Week Guidance from Your Recovery Coach

Earnie Larsen
with Carol Larsen Hegarty

Hazelden
Publishing

Hazelden Publishing
Center City, Minnesota 55012
hazelden.org/bookstore
800-328-9000

ISBN: 978-1-59285-828-6

Library of Congress Cataloging-in-Publication Data

Larsen, Earnest.
   Now that you're sober : week-by-week guidance from your recovery coach /
Earnie Larsen with Carol Larsen Hegarty.
      p. cm.
   ISBN 978-1-59285-828-6 (softcover)
1. Addicts--Rehabilitation--Handbooks, manuals, etc. I. Hegarty, Carol
Larsen, 1938- II. Title.
   HV4998.L37 2010
   616.86'103--dc22
                              2010008967

Editor's note
All names and stories used in this book have been altered to protect confidentiality.
This publication is not intended as a substitute for the advice of health care
professionals.
Alcoholics Anonymous, AA, and the Big Book are registered trademarks of Alcoholics
Anonymous World Services, Inc.

14   15   16   17   18   6   5   4   3   2   1

Cover design by David Spohn
Interior design by David Spohn
Typesetting by BookMobile Design and Publishing Services

Dedication

For Willard, the Eagle,
Sorely missed, never forgotten
And for "my guys" who honor me
With their friendship

Contents

Acknowledgments

I am grateful for the thousands of people who have taught me what is in this program—especially those of my team, who have most clearly shown me the face of God.

Introduction

To my dear sponsees,

Now That You're Sober is especially designed for those who are bravely moving through their first year of recovery—whether for the first or twentieth time. It is also for those who have been in recovery for much longer than a year but who find complacency creeping into their recovery efforts, who feel stuck and realize they need to recommit to the principles of recovery. For all of you, this book is a map that charts your way forward. Make no mistake about the intention of the guidance offered in this book. This is *not* just another "nice recovery book"—one that you read and then put aside, hopefully taking away a few good thoughts. My intention is that the material offered here be chewed, pulled apart, scrutinized, and internalized. This book is designed to be *worked*, preferably by two or more people together. It is intended to provide support, insights, and exercises that will *do something* about the high relapse rate of people starting recovery.

Only *doing* is doing, so I urge you to do the work. Obviously, the fifty-two weeks outlined in this text are meant to cover a year's worth of recovery, whenever that year starts. But digesting this material may take longer. You (and your group) may well not get through all the work suggested here in a year. Or, as the year goes on, you might feel called to return to some piece of work suggested here so you can take it to a new, deeper level that you weren't ready for earlier. That is perfectly acceptable. Spirit always seeks depth. Recovery is all about spirituality. Becoming "honest, open, and willing" often happens in stages.

Who am I to be writing such a book? Who am I to call myself your recovery coach? It is common for speakers in our Fellowship to qualify themselves as they begin speaking. They tell what gives them the right to stand up and command your attention. What qualifies a speaker in the Fellowship is never a college degree or fancy title. "Having been there" is the only qualification required. Is the speaker working a program? Has he or she stood in the trenches and made the tough decisions about quality of life? In this arena, titles are meaningless, experience is everything. So what qualifies me to dare call anyone my sponsee? Or more specifically to call you my sponsee? First of all, it is my forty-plus years of living life in the Fellowship. I've been around a long time. Second is the fact that, over all those years, I've coached, sponsored, pushed, pulled, coaxed, goaded, explained, ushered, held, and shepherded a good many people into recovery for the first time or back again into the Fellowship after a relapse. I've been there, sitting with you when children have died and been born, when your hearts were broken and when you found the strength to get up and try again, when you relapsed and when you reached milestones in your recovery. I was with you in times of despair—whether in prison, in treatment, in the hospital, in the rooms—as well as in those times when you fairly skipped in happiness down the red road of recovery.

I know both personally and through my connection to loved ones in recovery that this road called recovery is *tricky*. Old habits die hard. Some never do. They simply sit by the side of the road waiting for an opening so they can ambush us if we allow them entrance. I also know that "new" is often wobbly. Even a "new" that is a *good* new tests our hearts and minds. After perhaps living many years by the values that underpin the condition called "spiritual bankruptcy," change is difficult. If we try it alone, transformation is altogether beyond our powers. Yet that is what recovery asks and delivers if we work with others and remain faithful to its principles—not just change but *transformation*. The first step of transformation may come unbidden with blinding speed. For others, moving into recovery is less dramatic. Either way, the first step is free. It is given to us. But the rest of the journey must be earned through consistent effort, practicing a new way to be in this world. Learning new ways is difficult. Unfamiliar behaviors feel awkward. At first, many feel they are playacting in this new way. They say it feels odd or phony or rootless. Many are terrified that when the old urges of mind and body come clawing at them, they will cave in. They fear the deadly draw of the old way.

I know that many times in recovery, especially early on, there are tipping moments and turning points. There are moments when it is literally touch and go—when the hot breath of the beast blows in the tender face of new recovery from but inches away. I know that at those times especially, there is great need for a voice of hope and reason. This book can serve as that voice for you. I know at those times especially, there is great need for a presence to stand by your side while the beast prowls about. This book can serve as the presence for you. I know that at those times especially, there is great need for access to a protective shield to gather behind. This book can serve as that shield for you. I know that at those times especially, there is great need for a guide to show you the way through the jungle. This book can serve as your guide. So take this book with you on your journey of recovery and let me be one of your sponsors or recovery coaches.

Carry this book. Study it. Do the work on a daily basis. Follow the map laid out and share your work with others.

Every time a recovery action is taken, your spiritual bankroll grows. When the storm comes—and it will in one way or another—all will be well if your spiritual bankroll is larger than what must be withdrawn. The battle will be won. If the essential actions outlined here are *not* taken, however, your resources will be insufficient to deal with the need. It's as simple as that.

For my part, what I pledge to those of you who take this book with you to your first birthday is this: *I will always tell you the truth.* The truth may not always be popular or easy to accept or do—but it is the truth. And it is the truth that works. Others may find recovery on a different path than the Twelve Step Fellowship. I honor them. But my way has been the Twelve Step way, and I know that this program works for those who apply themselves to the principles outlined. I have felt it work. I have seen it work. I know what works because I stand on the shoulders of giants who have gone before and shown me and many thousands of others the way. *It will work for you.* No matter where you are starting from or how many times you may have started in the past, *it works if you work it.* With the encouragement and support in this book, you are not alone, no matter how powerfully old habits may call out to you. You are not without resources or strength. Come along with that great cavalcade of recovering people, millions strong, marching to that better place that seeks to embrace you. All of us hold out our hands to you, urging you to connect with us. There is nothing in this world more powerful than the Fellowship on the march. It is yours if you would have it. Words are shadows. The doing of the words is the substance behind the shadows. So, if you are ready, let us be up and doing. I will if you will.

> Your vest pocket sponsor and recovery coach,
> Earnie

SECTION 1

Getting Ready

• WEEK 1 •

Why Is a Portable Aftercare Program So Important?

The short answer is that aftercare is the antidote to relapse. People who plug into a solid aftercare program do not relapse—especially not in the all-important first year of recovery.

This is so because recovery from alcoholism and chemical dependency, especially for those with a dual diagnosis, is all about habit, repetition, and keeping the goal of recovery front and center in one's awareness. Relapse is never about the problems we all must deal with in everyday life. Problems happen. That's life. Relationships end or don't go the way we want, jobs disappoint, careers are lost, financial hardship may suddenly rear up its worrisome head. Problems come in all shapes and forms. Sometimes there seems to be no reason at all for the recurring urges that presage relapse. They just seem to pop up from some hidden source within ourselves.

Addicts, especially if their compulsion is magnified by a dual diagnosis of some form of depression, anxiety, or other mental illness, have learned to deal with these problems by escaping into their drug of choice. Retreating back into that drug feels as natural and necessary as breathing. Most have lived that way for a long time. *Addiction is the deepest form of habit.*

Recovery means learning a new way to live. Addicts learn that new way of life the same way they learned to find a temporary (and deceitful) answer to their problems by turning to alcohol and drugs. The habit of addiction permeates every aspect of a person's life: physical, mental, emotional, and spiritual.

Life's problems don't end with recovery. People fortunate enough to have had access to a formal treatment program were shielded from the press of daily problems and stresses in that intense, controlled environment. The basics of recovery were repeatedly presented until they became part of each person's core consciousness.

Others entered recovery through a different door than formal treatment. They came in under the power of a "First Step experience." (In truth, everyone enters recovery under the power of that First Step experience, however they get there.) Perhaps they simply got "sick and tired of being sick and tired." Or "enough was enough." Or the pain of staying where they were suddenly was more than the pain of doing something about the problem. The First Step experience goes by different names. Some call it a "tap on the shoulder." Others call it "hitting bottom" or "kissing concrete." Some people have amazing "white light" experiences where they seem to hear the voice of God speaking to them from the depth of their beings. For most, though, the tipping point that moves them into recovery is less dramatic. This experience has been called "conversion of an educational variety."

What was *your* original experience like? How would you describe it?

However people enter recovery, with whatever diagnosis, there comes a time when they either leave the facility they entered, or they find the initial push of the First Step experience wearing thin. The demands of "life on life's terms" break through whatever recovery honeymoon period they might have enjoyed. Problems start to crop up like bullies looking for a fight. It is at this moment that aftercare becomes critical.

Will these people remain faithful to all the imperatives they learned in treatment or from the old-timers they met "in the rooms"? Will they have the wisdom and the strength to keep moving down the recovery road? Or will the power of the old addictive thinking habits overpower newfound recovery and lure them into the back alley of addiction? How many might find a way to move through whatever problem life is serving up and use it as a brick in building the foundation of their new life?

The answer to those questions depends on the quality and continuity of the programs they work and whether they are working a solid aftercare program. If they "do the next right thing"—what they were taught to do when beset by problems, whether inner or outer—they will make it through and become stronger in their recovery. But if they forget those basic, lifesaving principles and don't do what they know they should, they will not survive. They will become another statistic racked up by relapse.

Again, no one relapses over exterior problems. People relapse because they haven't been faithful to their program; they've lost connection. Think about it. In times of problems and troubles, no matter what the diagnosis or severity of the urge, the ones who make it through are those who tighten up their programs and cling to them with even more determination.

Aftercare, whether focused on the first year of abstinence or on the tenth or twentieth birthday, is the practice of continually keeping those basics of recovery front and center in our awareness. It's following a set of procedures that helps us remember what that "next right thing" is. It's the how-to system of tapping into the support and wisdom of the Fellowship, whether at midday or the middle of the night. That's why aftercare is crucial. Aftercare is the antidote to relapse because it helps build and strengthen the new habits of recovery thinking and behavior.

Some wise old-timers warn, "Your addiction is out in the parking lot doing push-ups all the time you are working at your recovery. Your addiction isn't going anywhere. It's getting stronger as you learn to walk away from it." And it is. As the Big Book of AA tells us, the disease of addiction is "cunning, powerful, and baffling." And it's also infinitely patient—always waiting for an unguarded moment to pounce. Aftercare is what protects us at such moments.

MAKE IT REAL

I cannot overstress the importance of *doing the work*. (Remember that your addiction is out in the parking lot doing push-ups.) Doing the work goes a long way toward keeping it out in the parking lot.

ACTION STEPS

If you are one of the many who have trouble expressing your thoughts in writing, do the best you can. Before writing, say the words to yourself. Then give it your best shot. If you can't write a paragraph, write a sentence. If you can't write a sentence, write a few key words. The important thing is that you *do something*. The more you do, the greater the payoff.

WRITE: (two or three paragraphs, if you can, on the following topics. Give personal examples.)
1. What specific recovery behaviors do you need to practice to stay in recovery?
2. What specific recovery behaviors have you let slide in working your program?

SHARE: (with your group or sponsor) personal examples of times you allowed your feelings to dictate your behavior. Tell about a time when you
1. behaved angrily because you felt angry
2. behaved fearfully because you felt afraid
3. behaved hopelessly because you felt hopeless

• • •

• WEEK 2 •

How to Use This Book

When habit is the issue, repetition is king. People learn to live a life of addiction, and their teachers are many. Most often, addicts have practiced thinking addictive thoughts and acting out addictive behaviors for a good many years.

The same is true for a life in recovery. *Recovery is learned and it needs to be practiced.* The first movement into recovery is a gift. As mentioned in Week 1, recovery starts with a conversion experience of one kind or another. The result is a change in consciousness—even, in some sense, an alteration in personality. What was, no longer fits. You've been picked up and moved to a different psychic place.

The second movement into recovery must be *earned*. Many people have called that first dawning of recovery consciousness a miracle. Perhaps it is. But the power of miracles can fade. Through lack of attention and follow-through, the insight that was gained can wither and die. In contrast, nurturing the miracle is called "working your program."

Focus on the word *working*. There is nothing magical or miraculous about doing the work. *Program* means practice. And practice means keeping those basics of recovery that were learned in treatment (or from a counselor or through a sponsor and Big Book study group in a Twelve Step program) front and center in one's consciousness. That's what aftercare does. And that's what the program outlined in this book helps you to do—conveniently, simply, and comprehensively.

CONVENIENT

There are many reasons why a person new to recovery cannot plug into a traditional aftercare program—lack of time, money, or availability, for example. If this is the case with you, then you know what the reasons are.

The purpose of this portable aftercare book, or program, is to provide a course of action based on sound recovery principles practiced by millions of people over the years. All the important action steps, learning aids, and reminders in this book can be taken anywhere. I hope it becomes your "pocket sponsor" or "recovery coach," especially if you are new to recovery, if you are finding yourself slipping closer to a relapse and don't quite know why or what to do about it, or if you are dealing with a dual diagnosis or any other complicating issue. Whatever and wherever your starting point, the truths and actions suggested in this book are core truths. If your goal is to move successfully and serenely along the recovery road, the wisdom you need to remember and the actions suggested here are *necessary*.

Anyone, anytime can "work the program" by using the tools provided.

SIMPLE

Read the content and then do the action steps; it's as simple as that. But to get the maximum benefit of your efforts, *work with at least one other person*. Just as the first word in the Twelve Steps is *we*—and just as it is not possible to work an effective recovery program alone—any recovery effort shared doubles your benefits. Find someone else who wants to "work a better program." Then each of you—or the whole group, if that is the way you choose to use this book—may do the action steps and share what you learned from doing the work. A joy shared is doubled, and a problem not shared is also doubled.

A sizable group of people reviewed and "practiced" this book before it was put to paper. Several reported a curious finding. Many "'fessed up" that although all the weekly topics were important and the information relevant, what they actually did was hone in on a "favorite" topic or two. Perhaps it was one they had the most trouble with or one that caught their attention for whatever reason, so they "did the work" over and over. For them, this book may have become a critical resource manual for remembering what needs to be remembered. Do whatever works. If using the book in that way helps strengthen someone's recovery, so be it.

(Once you have used the book, we would welcome your feedback on how it has most helped you—see "About the Authors" on page 272.)

COMPREHENSIVE

The initial focus in writing this book was to safeguard people's journey to their first birthday. Yet no matter how many sober years or years of clean time have been racked up, the main reason for relapse is that people get sloppy with their program. They fail to guard the door, allowing the beast of addiction to come smashing through, red in tooth and claw. Relapse happens because the basics are "forgotten."

Many other topics might have been selected than the fifty-two chosen. But each topic discussed here is essential to recovery. In my forty-plus years of experience with and in recovery, these are the key elements or topics around which recovery is either gained or lost. If the suggested work in these pages is truly engaged—and thus the key elements of recovery are "remembered"—the first birthday will indeed be reached and, thanks to the program, so will many, many more.

ACTION STEPS

Okay—grab a pencil and paper or sit at your computer. It's time to dig a little deeper into this week's work by writing, sharing, and practicing.

WRITE: (Answer the questions as completely as possible.)
1. Look through the topics (page vi–vii) we will cover in our fifty-two weeks together. To you, which topics stand out as most important?
2. Why do these topics seem especially important to you?
3. Which topics do you think you might revisit again and again?

SHARE: (with your group or sponsor)
1. Describe any "troublemaker feelings" (self-pity, resentment, or others) that you're struggling with.
2. Express your gratitude for the help they are giving you and your continuing need of their ongoing support.

PRACTICE: Be part of the solution rather than the problem; introduce yourself to newcomers.

• • •

• WEEK 3 •

Dual Diagnosis

"Dual diagnosis," also described as "co-occurring" or "co-morbid," refers to being chemically dependent and having a secondary mental health issue. These mental health issues usually fall under the headings of depressive or anxiety disorders. Recently—and thankfully—more attention has been paid to the effects that childhood neglect or abuse issues have on the adult recovering person. The clinical designation of this form of mental illness is childhood onset PTSD (post-traumatic stress disorder).

Whatever the second disorder, several important facts must be considered when confronting a dual diagnosis.

1. No matter what the issue, or how unfair it may seem to those who are doubly afflicted, our literature assures us that "there is no situation too difficult to be made better." First and foremost, what's needed is *courage*. Don't give up. *Never* give up. No matter what, life can and will improve if a consistent program of daily discipline is embraced.

2. Recovery is not a competition. It is both misleading and dangerous to measure our insides against someone else's outsides. So it doesn't matter if one person seems to have an easier road to recovery than someone else. The *only* thing that counts is that each of us accepts the cards we're dealt and play them with all the energy and commitment we can muster.

3. No matter what the diagnosis, honestly sharing one's truth is what moves a person out of isolation. Isolation is the

enemy. It is in isolation that one's problems fester and become unmanageable. All of us must honestly learn to "tell on" whatever is troubling us.

4. Appropriately prescribed medications from a professional familiar with addiction medicine are a gift of our time. Anyone who claims that medications obtained and used in the context of responsible medical practice is contrary to working a good recovery program is plain *wrong*. The founders of AA make it abundantly clear that "more will be revealed." And as time has passed, new medical developments can now offer great help to many suffering alcoholics and other chemically dependent people. The founders had such a clear grasp of the pain and wreckage caused by addiction that they were willing to try any new procedure or discovery that would legitimately relieve the suffering. Many of our number would no doubt have died long ago, and/or caused immeasurably more pain and suffering to others, without the relief afforded by appropriate medications.

We encourage all who think they may be helped in their recovery efforts by medications to network in their meetings with those who have found such help already. Certain medications are more user-friendly to addicts, and certain medical professionals are more skilled and understanding of the addict's unique situation. By all means, find such professionals and in no way feel guilty or "less than" others because medications not needed by others may help you. Nothing in recovery is more important than first reaching sobriety and then staying sober by moving into "living the solution," which is increasing the spiritual dimension of our lives.

5. *Accept what cannot be changed.* This means accepting that dual diagnosis issues tend to magnify the already turbulent mental and emotional state of an addict. As one dually diagnosed recovering person put it, "My blues are bluer and my reds are redder." We can't really know how blue another's blue is or how red their reds are, but the inescapable truth is that we all have to play with the cards that are dealt us.

Most people bravely walking the recovery road with a dual diagnosis tell similar stories. They are sick and tired of having to carry such a heavy load. They dread the slide into depression or the unchecked manic quality that at times pervades their lives. They hate feeling jittery and anxious so often, let alone having to endure outright anxiety attacks. Those suffering with childhood onset PTSD understandably bewail their constant sense of disassociation, their lack of any sense of safety, and their consistently exaggerated response to circumstances that in reality are rather minor events.[1] But therein lies the rub—*reality*. What is "real" for one may well not be for another.

No matter what the situation, however, acceptance without resentment is the gateway to serenity. What is, is. When people grow through whatever initial resentment and denial they may feel toward the cards life dealt them, they are able to move into blessed acceptance. And once the medicine of acceptance is applied to whatever inner wound remains unhealed, people discover that although diligent effort still needs to be applied to the situation, *the situation is no longer in control of their lives.* That is healing. The issue doesn't disappear once and for all, but it no longer has the power to control their lives.

MAKE IT REAL

1. If you labor under a dual diagnosis in recovery, and were to rate the level that you accept your situation without resentment, what grade would you give yourself on a scale of 1 to 10? _____

2. If you were to rate how well and consistently you "tell on your situation" with vigorous honesty, what grade would you give yourself? _____

---

[1] For a fuller treatment of childhood onset PTSD, consult *Destination Joy: Moving Beyond Fear, Loss, and Trauma in Recovery,* a Hazelden book by Earnie Larsen.

A C T I O N   S T E P S

How are your action steps going? Are you able to complete all the writing and sharing steps? *Do what you can do.* If a task seems too much, cut it in half. If that seems too much, then cut that in half again. The *direction* you are going is much more important than your pace. Even a small step is a thousand times better than no step at all. You can follow one little step with another, and another . . . all the way home.

WRITE: (two or three paragraphs, or whatever you are able, on the following topics. Use personal examples.)

1. If you have a dual diagnosis, describe how that complicates your recovery efforts.
2. Reflect on how you rated yourself on the acceptance scale in this week's reading. What are the consequences—positive or negative—of how you have accepted the cards you've been dealt?

SHARE: (with your group or sponsor) what most helps you to deal with your dual diagnosis.

PRACTICE: Everyone needs and wants to "belong." The next time newcomers are introduced at a meeting, pay attention so you can greet them by name.

●   ●   ●

The Nature of Addiction

• WEEK 4 •

Begin at the Beginning

Okay, now that the decks have been cleared for action in the first three weeks of this program, let's push on with the work. Where to start? Well, why not the beginning? For an alcoholic/addict, that is always at the same place—at the pain and misery that addiction causes. Active addiction hurts—in fact, it creates suffering that goes beyond the power of words to adequately describe. If anyone should ask, "Why should I do all the work recovery demands? What's my motivation?" The answer is this: *remember how much your addiction hurt.* If you don't do the work, your addiction will make you bleed through a thousand wounds all over again.

• • •

Marcus relapsed. He went out and "did more research," as the saying goes. What he found out is that active addiction hurts every time. Luckily, he was allowed back into the long-term treatment program he relapsed out of. As was the custom at this facility, upon his return he was asked to address the rest of the folks in the program and tell them what he had learned. The following is pretty close to what he said: *I failed to remember the pain that addiction costs me. The cost goes up each time I relapse. What happened was—I forgot. I forgot the price I would pay.*

Think of your own last relapse or the relapse of someone you know. What happened? How did the relapse get started? What is the lesson?

Forgetting the cost of relapse isn't like forgetting a telephone number. What Marcus was talking about was getting careless and complacent about his recovery. He was forgetting what addiction cost him when he allowed himself to fall under its power once again. The nature of addiction is suffering, pain, loss, waste, and tragedy.

No one relapses without first forgetting the cost.

If you doubt this, think back to the worst moment in your addiction. Recall that moment when, finally, "enough was enough"—when you'd lost more than you could bear to throw away. How motivated were you to be done with addiction at that blessed moment? Did you see the look on your children's faces and realize they had lost faith in you? Could you see that they had given up counting on you?

Perhaps your "moment" occurred when, handcuffed and wearing an orange jumpsuit, you stood before the judge awaiting your sentence. You realized you hadn't looked in a mirror for years just because you had no respect for the image you would see there. Perhaps you turned over in bed and woke up next to someone whose name you didn't know.

Whatever your moment was, remember what it was like and ask yourself if *anything* is worth going back to that point of pain. There is the reason to do the work recovery requires: "I will *not* do that to myself and my loved ones again!" As you work through this book, you will be asked repeatedly to return to this point of pain. Why? Because right there is the choice. Either return to hell or stay the course of the marathon that recovery is.

M A K E   I T   R E A L

Do this piece of work. Do it for yourself. Take the time to make the cost of relapse *conscious.* Face the beast. In as much detail as possible, write out the cost of your addiction relative to

_____ self-esteem	_____ health
_____ family	_____ friendship
_____ financial issues	_____ serenity
_____ legal issues	_____ spirituality

Do not hurry through this assignment. Write out your experience in as much detail as you can. See it. Feel it. Taste it. Touch it. Make it as real as possible. Then, if you can, share what you have written with another who's working through this book. Remember that whatever you share will have double the power. Then, when you have clarified for yourself what is at stake and how much skin you have on the table, write a letter to your addiction. Reflect on the cost. Think hard about it. What do you have to say to and about managing a condition that has taken so much from you? When you've done that, keep this letter, read it on a regular basis, and share it with trusted others.

Now, ask yourself again: Is it worth the effort to work a focused, consistent program? When you consider the consequences, is *anything* more important?

ACTION STEPS

The ideas in this week's reading are key. So please *don't skip* this exercise in digging deeper. You will reap immense benefits by doing the work suggested here. Clarify the stakes at risk in your recovery. Write out the cost and keep it close at hand.

WRITE: (two or three paragraphs—or whatever you can do—on the following topics. Give personal examples.)
1. Estimate of the cost of your addiction in any of the specific areas listed in this week's reading.
2. Think about what you have to say to something that has cost you and your loved ones so much. Write a letter to your addiction.

SHARE: (with your group or sponsor) an example of the worst moment of your addiction.

CONSCIOUS CONTACT: Ask your Higher Power for the strength to get honest with yourself about all that your addiction has taken from you.

• • •

• WEEK 5 •

Alcoholism/Drug Addiction
Is an Incurable, Fatal, Progressive Disease

While keeping the stakes you are playing for firmly in mind (the work you did in Week 4), let's move on to another fundamental truth about the nature of addiction. *Addiction has a life of its own that lies in wait to destroy us and everyone we love.* As one Twelve Step member said, "All our addiction needs is a crack in the door, an unguarded moment to storm back into our lives again"—bringing with it all the suffering and misery that we shone a light on in Week 4.

Most of us have had fun debating topics such as the merits of different sports teams or political positions far into the night. Seldom is anyone's mind changed. After all the argument, the parties usually go their own ways, holding pretty much the same opinions they had in the first place.

Sometimes, however, different viewpoints are more than just "sport"—they are worthy of serious consideration. Suppose a person is diagnosed with a serious illness. The interpretation of an X-ray could help decide the best next step in caring for the patient, so input from several doctors is crucial.

But there really isn't *any* room for discussion about some issues. Either the truth is accepted, or a major catastrophe is set in motion. Would you discuss whether or not it's a good idea for a child to play with a loaded gun? While the foolish debate goes on, the child may well blow his or her head off.

The same is true with the grim realities of addiction. It is a fact that addiction to alcohol or any other hard-core drug is a fatal disease. Challenging this truth invites disaster.

Do you have any doubts that your addiction is a fatal disease? Have you entertained slippery thoughts such as "Maybe I'm cured now" or "Just one drink won't hurt"? Or perhaps you've slipped back into one of these expressions of pre-recovery delusion and denial: "No one tells me what to do." "I'll drink if I want to drink." Or the ever-popular "I'm not hurting anyone else. It's none of their business if I drink or not."

Indulging in this form of "stinking thinking" is as dangerous as giving a child a loaded gun to play with. Would you drive your car one hundred miles an hour knowing full well that the brakes were bad? Only a fool with a death wish would do such a thing. By the same token, only someone in the grip of an addiction would play around with life-threatening thoughts of using again.

Alcoholism/addiction *is* a fatal disease—and it's one without mercy that can never be cured. It doesn't care about your well-being. Mess with it, and it will kill you without a second thought. Addiction, in fact, is like an extreme terrorist who not only can, but *wants* to destroy you and everything you love. It has destroyed millions of lives before you were ever born. And it awaits any chance—the slightest opening of the door—to come barging into your life and through you, to threaten your children down to the seventh generation.

There are some people, I know, who would call such language about addiction "extreme." They'd say it's narrow-minded thinking and old-fashioned. They are wrong. A fatal disease is a fatal disease no matter what new theory or paradigm comes into fashion. *We must never forget.*

Some people warn that "anything you name, you claim." They argue that the more you keep reminding yourself that you are addicted to alcohol and/or drugs, the more you attach yourself to the addiction.

In some situations, this makes sense. For countless recovering addicts, though—especially in our first year of recovery—*it is crucial that we never forget the fatal nature of the disease we carry.* Look out behind the barn. See the mile-high pile of bodies stacked up out there. Those are people who played with (or at least didn't take seriously enough) the fatal nature of their addiction.

There's an important distinction between addiction to alcohol and drugs and any other disease. *Addiction destroys a person's character.* Why does it murder the spirit? Because addictions lie. They never stop trying to put lies in the driver's seat of a life. In fact, the very lifeblood of addiction is delusion and denial. Addiction is downright *insanity.* Take your eye off that fact, and disaster is sure to follow.

Have you relapsed before? What lie blew a hole in your decision-making ability? How "harmless" and even "right" did that lie appear to be as you slid down the slippery chute of relapse?

Take your eye off your addiction, and it will kill you. End of story.

Want to bring the fatal nature of this disease into even clearer focus? Think about your past. Make a short list of the hellish, shameful, disastrous, terrible situations you created for yourself and those you love during your active addiction. (All those who died in their addiction, of course, won't have a chance to make such a list. Their addiction killed them.)

How clear does the meaning of the word *fatal* have to be to command your attention? What behavior will addicts *not* use to procure and protect their source?

• • •

Consider the lengths these addicts went to for their drugs and where their use brought them.

Brent, an up-and-coming salesman for a high-tech company, padded his expense reports to cover his out-of-town drug purchases. When questioned about his excessive spending on "entertainment," Brent was nervously defensive. His boss's suspicions were confirmed after checking with two of Brent's clients. Tearfully telling his wife that he'd been fired, Brent said, "It all went up my nose."

Under the influence, Ross slipped back into his house after his wife and daughter had left for work and school. His only concern was to find money for another bottle. He was willing to steal and hock the TV set, the silverware, his wife's jewelry (he'd already hocked his own wedding ring). All he could find today was the money his daughter had collected from selling her Girl Scout cookies. He took it without a second thought.

Angela simply said she got tired of waking up without even knowing the name of the man sleeping next to her.

MAKE IT REAL

Remember where you've been. *Never* minimize or brush aside the depths that addiction will gladly take you to if you mess around with it. Use every ounce of the weight of guilt, shame, and fear your addiction has already caused you to shore up your motivation. Ask yourself: What was the worst time in your active addiction? How willing are you to relive that time—and worse? What are you willing to do to prevent all that pain and suffering? Every day, promise yourself *never again*. Why? Because if you never forget, you will never return.

ACTION STEPS

Don't stop now. Doing the reading but failing to take the action steps is like working all week but failing to pick up your paycheck. Think about what can be gained by doing these action steps. Do whatever you can do, but *do something*.

WRITE: (two or three paragraphs, or whatever you can do. Give personal examples.)

Make a short list of the hellish, shameful, disastrous, terrible situations you created for yourself (and those you love) during your active addiction. Don't sugarcoat your examples; your addiction surely doesn't.

SHARE: (with your group or sponsor) how you rationalized your drinking/drug use in the past.

REACH OUT: Exchange phone numbers with someone in your group whose story is similar to yours.

• • •

• WEEK 6 •

Sobriety Must Be the First Priority

Once you get out of treatment—or past the first rigorous weeks or months of beginning recovery through a Twelve Step program—the intensity of your program may begin to lighten up. This is a relief for many program newcomers, who felt a bit guilty over taking time away from work or family responsibilities as they focused so intently on recovery. You return to the "real" world, and soon life gets busy once again—the demands on your time pile up like snow against a fence in a blizzard. Many, many people who relapse after a good start look back and claim their problem was that they just "didn't have time" for aftercare.

Stay strong. Stay vigilant. There can be no such thing as "I don't have time for aftercare." For a recovering alcoholic/addict, there is nothing and no one that can come before sobriety. Though the time commitment and intensity of the program may decrease, *nothing* must crowd out the primary importance of working a focused, effective program.

• • •

John was certain that he understood the nature of alcoholism and addiction. He knew that it was a killer without mercy or remorse, but now that he was out of treatment, he had bills to pay. He said he'd put his family in a terrible financial mess, and he owed it to them to turn that situation around as quickly as possible. Being a natural-born salesman, that meant he had to hit the road, and hit it hard.

That *sounds* reasonable, doesn't it? Who can be faulted for being responsible? Isn't that part of recovery—making amends by "letting it begin with me"? How could John do anything but run as fast as he could to make up for all the time he'd lost?

But how did this good intention actually play out? Before long, John no longer had time for regular meetings, and he certainly was too busy for anything like regular contact with a sponsor. And that wasn't all. Making sales sometimes called for shading the truth. "Every salesperson does it," John told himself, and John did it better than most. Before long, "shading the truth" turned into outright lying. "Rigorous honesty" fell out of his life like something he could no longer afford. In no time at all, he was "mentally drunk," and physical drunkenness always comes close on the heels of mental drunkenness. John was heading into relapse.

As it turned out, John was lucky. He got a second chance. (Actually, he'd tell you it was about his *tenth* chance.) When he finally came back to his meetings, he poured out the guilt and shame he felt over letting everyone down. Then an old-timer asked him, "So what did you gain by letting something come before your sobriety?"

• • •

In the early AA literature, "doing what it takes" meant not only staying clean and sober, but also moving into the life of the Promises—which meant faithfully doing one's "daily disciplines." Each of those words is precious and powerful.

Daily, of course, means *every* day. And in recovery, it doesn't take long before you realize that every day sometimes means every hour, or every half hour, or sometimes every ten seconds. It means as often as it takes. It means committed. It means all the way in. It means "all it takes is all there is."

Disciplines means those actions that must be taken whether you feel like it or not. Your program never asks, "How are you feeling?" It asks, "How are you doing?" Only *doing* is doing. "Thinking about" is not doing. "Planning for" is not doing. "Feeling" surely is not doing. *Only doing is doing.*

Early in recovery, lots of people groan when they hear such talk. It all seems so hard. Working a good program seems like such an effort.

And it seems like it's going to take so long. *For the rest of my life?* Often, the spirit falters.

But program wisdom tells us that keeping on the path "for the rest of my life" can only happen one day at a time. When the rubber hits the highway, it means "just for today." You don't have to and should not look down the many years of the rest of your life. All you have to do is look at today. Just for today, am I willing to put my sobriety *first?* Am I willing to do what that takes *just for today?* Who knows about tomorrow? Tomorrow isn't here yet, and for all we know, it may never come. So the real question is "Am I willing to put sobriety first for just this minute, for this hour, for this day?"

Daily means today. *Disciplines* means *do it*. It means *act*. It means put your muscles in motion. It means do the next right thing. That's all. Not the next right thing for the next ten or twenty years. It means right here, right now, today. Are you willing to do the next right thing for the sake of the rewards you will gain by doing so?

> *The rewards are not only real—they're better than anything you can imagine at the start of your recovery journey.*

People become what they practice. What once, at the start of recovery, may have seemed burdensome and difficult will become natural. Going to meetings becomes comfortable and enjoyable. Sponsors become dear friends. Honesty and gratitude become the air breathed by the soul. Humility becomes the heartbeat of the spirit. Service to others becomes a priority and a privilege. A life other than one built on the values of recovery becomes unthinkable. Your new life becomes the most precious thing you have to bequeath to the loved ones coming along behind you.

● ● ●

Ellen was new to recovery and the life that recovery is. Her addiction had dragged her into the darkness—far from positive realities such as fellowship and community, honesty and responsibility, joy and serenity. She thought such things were far beyond her reach. But the gift of recovery opened up before her when she dipped her toe into the sacred water and got started. Early in her recovery, she attended an AA conference. (Actually, she was virtually dragged there by her sponsor.) What she found there was amazing. For the life of her, she couldn't believe these people were drunks and addicts. They were having such fun—and none of them were drunk or high! She watched them laughing and joking among themselves. They seemed to be truly at ease with themselves and each other. Was this possible? Could drug and alcohol addicts really be like this? Could *she* ever be like this?

Her sponsor read her like a book. Ellen went to bed that night with her sponsor's words dancing in her head: *If you want what we have, do what we do.*

• • •

Above all, that means *sobriety first*. There is no such thing as not having time to work an aftercare program to your first birthday—and many more.

ACTION STEPS

Here is another essential crossroads in the recovery journey. Either sobriety and ongoing recovery is primary—coming before everything else—or it isn't. If it isn't, addiction wins sooner or later. *It is critical to recovery that sobriety always remains our primary concern.* No secondary goal must be allowed to come first.

WRITE: Review the list of "secondary goals" below. Then write two or three paragraphs—or as much as you can—about the goal or goals that you might be tempted to put ahead of recovery.

- finding or keeping a job
- getting ahead at work
- finding the perfect (or any) relationship
- reconciling with family
- making money
- "catching up" for all you have lost

SHARE: (with your group or sponsor) some danger signs in your life that might warn that a secondary goal is coming ahead of sobriety.

REACH OUT: After a meeting, thank someone whose sharing was especially helpful to you.

CONSCIOUS CONTACT: Ask your Higher Power for the willingness to "do the disciplines."

• • •

Problems Aren't the Problem

Being in recovery doesn't mean a problem-free life. Life is still life. Problems are part of everyone's life. Many troubles that befall people seem to be extremely harsh and unfair. So what are newly recovering people supposed to do when problems seem to gut them—especially the "undeserved" kind of problems?

Warning: *Unrealistic expectations* easily slip unnoticed into a newly recovering person's thinking. They are a form of "stinking thinking." One of these unrealistic expectations concerns problems. It's easy to entertain thoughts such as "After all the changes I've made, don't I deserve a bit of immunity from bad luck?" Or "Now that I've turned my life around, shouldn't people more or less forgive the debts I've piled up with them?" Or the ever-popular "Since I'm working a program in the here and now, I shouldn't have to deal with any—or at least not too many—consequences from my using life."

Few would readily admit that they think this way. When spoken aloud, such thoughts seem clearly wrong. But they are not spoken aloud and so are not on our radar—they simply slip into a recovering person's consciousness. And since frustration is always relative to expectations, the more unrealistic your thinking, the more frustrated you become. In that first precious, critical year of the recovery journey, unchecked frustration is often the open manhole of relapse.

Problems happen. Difficulties of all kinds *will* be part of that first year of recovery. To understand and *accept* that fact is an important hedge against allowing them to do you in. Working a recovery program is not about avoiding all problems (except the time bombs a using addict constantly plants in his or her own life). The promise of working a program in recovery is that you will now have new and better tools to handle the "slings and arrows" that inevitably come to all of us in this imperfect world.

No one has ever relapsed over problems. Problems do not cause relapse. What causes relapse is a lack of body armor (program practices) when you're under fire.

In other words, *relapse is caused by failing to work a focused enough program before problems come your way.*

• • •

These days, Mary calls herself "a grateful recovering alcoholic." Now fifty-three years old, she is a suburban housewife who's had an on-again off-again history of use (relapse—back into the program—relapse—get up and try again).

At a recent open meeting, she shared the main truth that the journey of her life had taught her: "I have to work my program every day, no matter what. Because that 'what' has never been far from my door."

After five years of mostly clean and sober living, Mary was diagnosed with colon cancer. She said that she found this "terribly unfair," especially since she'd tried her best in those five years to be of service to others. She said she figured the Big Guy Upstairs owed her a break because she'd been doing so much for others in recovery.

Feeling betrayed by God (and life and recovery), she admitted that she went out on "one hell of a bender." But "thanks to the gift of finally waking up," she described how she "pulled her head out of a dark, smelly place" and crawled back to the program on her knees.

"The most amazing thing," she said, was this realization: "All those years I thought I was working my program just to keep me from drinking. I had no idea what I was really doing was working my program to deal with the giant curve ball that life was going to throw at me years down the line."

Then Mary shared this saying: "When a storm hits, a bird stays safe by moving its nest closer to the trunk of the tree." Since it seemed there was always a storm of some kind in her life, Mary figured out that she needed her nest close to the tree trunk *every* day. She needed her life focused on recovery.

• • •

Ron was a street hustler. Most people would probably call him a street "thug," but he prefers to think of himself as a "hustler." He did drugs, made drugs, sold drugs, and practiced every other hateful act that goes with "living the life." When he introduces himself at a meeting, Ron says he is addicted to "the life" rather than to any specific mood-altering substance. He says that he was so evil that when he died, Satan would be forced to give up his throne to him.

"But my Higher Power had other ideas," Ron quickly adds. In that beyond-belief way that First Steps happen, Ron received his "tap on the shoulder." In "a moment of clarity," he enrolled in a nine-month live-in treatment program. For more than six months, the miracle of his changing life continued in treatment. Then he hit a problem.

Someone stole something from a resident's room, and Ron was blamed. He didn't do it, and he said so, but he was ejected from the program anyway. Rather than melt back into his old enemy ("the life"), he held firm to the tenets of his program. He moved his nest closer to the trunk of the tree. The result? Today he is much more than clean and sober. Now he is living the life of the Promises.

MAKE IT REAL

Everyone has problems—some serious, some less so, some partly or wholly our fault, and some not. So what? The point isn't whether you are or are not experiencing problems. Whether you're on the mountain or in the valley isn't the point, either. The point is that no matter where you are—especially in that first year of recovery—whether dually diagnosed or not, *what kind of program are you working?* How close to the tree trunk have you moved your nest? Problems are not the problem. *Weak programs are the problem.* If your nest is close to the trunk of the tree, no wind in the world can blow it away.

A C T I O N   S T E P S

Remember that addictions are sneaky. They worm their way into ongoing recovery a tiny bit at a time. When they get far enough in, it is too late! Recovery demands vigilance. But to be vigilant, you must first understand what it is that you must guard against.

What kinds of problems cause you to work a sloppy program or to stop altogether? Do this piece of work so you can understand what you must be vigilant about.

WRITE: (two or three paragraphs, or whatever you can do)
  1. What problems would you likely allow to knock you out of your recovery?
  2. What problems have done so in the past?

SHARE: (with your group or sponsor) examples of "stinking thinking" you're now ready to admit.

REACH OUT: Give what you want to get. Be alert to opportunities to help out when a friend or loved one needs help.

CONSCIOUS CONTACT: Ask your Higher Power to help you "keep first things first."

• • •

Getting the Problem Right

• WEEK 8 •

If We Get the Problem Wrong,
We'll Never Get the Solution Right

What's our problem? As quickly and honestly as you can, write down or say out loud, "My problem is _____." Did you say drugs or alcohol? If you did, it's the wrong answer. How you complete that all-important statement matters. *Someone who hasn't clearly identified the problem will not be able to take effective action against it.* Does that sound like an overstatement? If so, I'd like you to meet three friends of mine.

• • •

Charles has the dubious distinction of having entered more treatment centers than anyone I know. His total is forty-nine times, although he'll be the first to admit that he didn't *finish* forty-nine treatment programs. He got admitted that many times. At the meeting where he was given his three-year clean and sober medallion, he said, "Every time I worked my program just to stay sober, it never worked. Nothing worked until I finally figured out that I had to change *me*. My problem was *me*, not just alcohol and drugs. I must have heard that a thousand times during all my years of using. But when I finally *heard* it—and did something about it— my life in recovery began." Then he did a cool thing. He held up an ordinary-looking key and told us a story. In his using days, his mother wouldn't let him in the house. When he called to say he was coming, she'd put food out on the porch. After eating, he was told to leave the plate there and get on down the road. Holding up the key, Charles told us that his mother had recently given him this house key. "Come in and sit down any time you want," she'd added. His life in recovery didn't get started until he finally figured out what the problem was.

● ● ●

Tom's story is much the same. At this same meeting, he was also being awarded his three-year sober medallion. Tom said he was a rookie as far as formal treatment went—at least compared to Charles. He had spent time in only thirteen treatment programs. He said that his "moment of clarity" was when the truth finally dawned on him: "I realized that first I had to take care of the alcohol. But then I had to take care of the guy drinking all that alcohol." While still in high school, Tom's first incarceration was thirty days for driving under the influence. "Some kids get summer breaks. I got thirty days behind bars," he said. For the next twenty-five years, it was in and out of prison and in and out of recovery.

Tom didn't have a house key to hold up, but he did read us a letter from his thirteen-year-old daughter. In part, it said how proud she was of him and how glad she was that he had "found himself" so he could finally be her dad and she could be his daughter. With tears in his eyes, Tom told us how blessed his life was now—as long as he dealt with the addict and not just the booze and drugs.

● ● ●

Peggy has been diagnosed with both chemical dependency and bipolar disorder. She says her situation is like a "toxic bowl of snakes"— meaning it's hard to figure where one condition starts and the other one ends. "Like a strawberry that's both red and sweet," Peggy says she is totally both. In her at least, one condition does not exist without the other. She says she has to pay close attention to both problems because either one of them can take her down. Where they cross each other, she says, is that all the work that helps her deal with her bipolar condition is much the same work that keeps her clean and sober. Her bipolar disorder, for example, requires her to closely monitor her moods, practice rigorous honesty about what is going on inside herself, and stay connected to what she calls her "trinity of power"—God, self, and other human beings. "I am not my problems," she says. "I am a human being who is more than my problems, so I have to pay attention to what's going on inside myself and to take action when action is necessary—which is always."

• • •

No one is saying it is okay to be soft on abstinence. *Abstinence must always come first.* (Revisit Week 6.) The question, though, is how to achieve uninterrupted abstinence. As you gain more time in recovery, focusing only on abstinence is not enough—it is putting a Band-Aid on the real problem. Rather, we need to begin focusing on the person who has the problem—which will, in turn, take us to the cause of "the problem." This is where we can do our best work. The key idea here is that alcohol and drugs are not "the problem." *We* are the problem. (A later week will discuss how we are also the solution.)

MAKE IT REAL

One of the best ways to learn anything is to teach it. How can that be? What we can't explain, we don't know well enough. So, explain to another (in your own words, using your own experiences) why "It isn't the alcohol or drugs that are the problem. The person using the alcohol and drugs is the problem." Explain it until the concept makes perfect sense to you. When the explanation is as comfortable to you as your old house slippers, it is time to take this truth to a deeper, more personal, and more specific level. Are you ready to move on?

ACTION STEPS

Recovery is all about stepping up and showing up—going on whether you're in the valley or on the mountaintop. It's about the willingness to keep looking at strange-sounding ideas until they start to make sense. "Getting the problem right" is one good example. Many find it difficult to go beyond fixating on the chemical as "the problem." Do the work suggested here to be sure you understand what the real problem is.

WRITE: (two or three paragraphs—or whatever you can do—on each of the following topics. Use personal examples.)
1. Explain what Charles, Tom, and Peggy (in this week's reading) were talking about. What point were they making?
2. Explain how that same point is true for you.

SHARE: (with your group or sponsor) ways in which *you* (not the alcohol or drugs) have been your biggest problem.

CONSCIOUS CONTACT: Humbly ask God to grant you the wisdom to know the difference between you and your use of drugs.

• • •

• WEEK 9 •

Spiritual Bankruptcy

Both the Big Book and the "Twelve and Twelve" (*Twelve Steps and Twelve Traditions*) make clear that "the problem" is *us* rather than the alcohol or drugs we used. They explain this basic truth in many ways, but the description I like best is "spiritual bankruptcy." Why? Because spiritual bankruptcy is at the heart of every alcoholic/addict's problem and the cause of all the dreadful loss and tragedy that addiction causes (revisit Week 4). This definition fits perfectly with the basic Twelve Step approach of understanding addiction and recovery as a disease that cannot be cured but can be arrested. We've all heard in meetings that there is no cure for the disease of alcoholism, but that we are given a reprieve on a twenty-four-hour basis contingent on our spiritual condition. If our spiritual condition is "bankrupt"—if we have no "spiritual bankroll" (revisit the Introduction)—then, obviously, we will not be granted that all-important reprieve. If we will not do what it takes to keep ourselves out of spiritual bankruptcy, we will miss out on the second chance that is so freely given by a loving Higher Power.

But what exactly *is* spiritual bankruptcy? Somehow these words sound theoretical. They lend themselves to intellectualization and the kind of endless (and mostly mindless) philosophical speculation that many of our kind tend to engage in. And as long as we keep the term "out there," we cannot access its meaning. So what happens? By disregarding the meaning as mere theory, we blindly walk into the lion's den with our eyes shut.

But spiritual bankruptcy isn't theory. It isn't "out there." To grasp its meaning, return to the work you did in Week 4. Feel again and see again what you lost to your disease. Remember again the look on your children's faces when they lost faith in you. Recall what it felt like to be cuffed, shackled, and hauled before a judge. Remember again the terrible self-contempt you felt during your using years. Take out your letter to your addiction. Read it again. *That isn't theory.* Look closely into the mirror of your addiction. *What you are looking at is spiritual bankruptcy.*

The best way to understand spiritual bankruptcy is to study your dominant thoughts and behaviors in your using years. What values was your life based on during your active addiction? Those values are the skeleton, the heartbeat, and the flowing blood of spiritual bankruptcy.

So let's do the work. Think, reflect, ponder, pray—and then write. (Of course, it's not easy. No one said this kind of work is easy. Recovery is not easy, but it is possible. Only you can decide if you are worthy of living your life in the solution rather than in the problem.)

What does your list of spiritually bankrupt values look like? Here are the top six reported by hundreds of our brothers and sisters at this point of their recovery journey. Do yours match up with these? Some of the pitiful values that underlie active addiction include the following:

1. EGO: Me, me, me—only me. It's *all* about me!
2. INSTANT GRATIFICATION: I want what I want, and I want it *now.*
3. ONLY FEELINGS COUNT: If I feel like it, I do it.
4. DISHONESTY: To get what I want, I'll tell anyone anything.
5. TOTAL RELIANCE ON SELF: I am God.
6. IRRESPONSIBILITY: Hit, hide, or run when things get tough.

Now, choose three of these or any other negative values that jump out at you. Take all the time you need to write out several *specific* examples of how you acted out these values in the spiritually bankrupt life of addiction. On the next page, list the three "values" you selected and check them off after you have written detailed examples of how you acted out each value.

_____ Value 1: _____

_____ Value 2: _____

_____ Value 3: _____

MAKE IT REAL

READER ALERT: *The following point is critical.*

What's the fundamental problem created by living these values? What are the consequences of these values? What difference does it make? The bottom line is that living these values results in *isolation*. And isolation is the key element of spiritual bankruptcy. Why? Because spiritual bankruptcy breaks your connection to your Higher Power, self, and other human beings. Loss of connection is both the cause and the consequence of spiritual bankruptcy. *No one ever relapses without first severing honest connections with God, self, and others.* Spiritual bankruptcy *is* the loss of connection that makes relapse inevitable.

Next week, we'll consider one more aspect of getting the problem right. As unflattering and disagreeable as it might be, that aspect is the insanity of addiction.

ACTION STEPS

Here we come to another key concept: What is spiritual bankruptcy? It's central to your recovery to understand what this means—both generally and specifically—in your life. Give yourself the gift of doing the work.

WRITE: (two or three paragraphs—or whatever you can do—on the following topic. Give personal examples.)

Review the three negative values you identified as underpinning your spiritual bankruptcy, as described in the reading. Then explain as best you can how acting out these negative values creates spiritual bankruptcy.

SHARE: (with your group or sponsor) specific examples of how living these values created isolation (also called "the hole in the soul") in your life.

PRACTICE: Write or call a friend or family member with whom you've lost connection.

CONSCIOUS CONTACT: Ask your Higher Power to deliver you from spiritual bankruptcy.

• • •

• WEEK 10 •

The Insanity of Addiction

It's not politically correct to use the term *insanity* these days. In fact, calling someone insane is enough to get you immediately thrown out of Politically Correct International! Yet no alcoholic/addict in recovery whom I've ever known had a problem admitting that his or her life in active addiction was *insane.* Everyone on a Twelve Step walk accepts the "disease" definition of alcoholism and addiction. You probably know that it was named as such by the American Medical Association in 1956. Alcoholism/addiction is also listed in the American Psychiatric Association's manual of recognized mental illnesses. Alcoholism/addiction can be understood as a disease in several different ways. All are helpful, and all are correct. This week's work, however, focuses on just one aspect of addiction as a disease: *Addicts in active addiction are living a very real form of insanity. For all practical purposes, they are not sane while drinking or using.*

That's what the second of the Twelve Steps clearly tells us: "Came to believe that a Power greater than ourselves could restore us to sanity." If people need to be "restored," clearly they have lost something of enormous value. In this case, the step is talking about sanity.

An alcoholic/addict's self-talk always makes sense, no matter how crazy it is. That's why alcoholics/addicts, especially in early recovery, cannot be the sole judge of what's reasonable and logical. "Insane" people are not able to accurately interpret reality. As the Big Book says, their thinking is flawed.

Once again, connect the dots. Get the problem right so you can also get the solution right (Week 8). Work with these ideas until the connection between them becomes clear. Addiction is the deepest form of habit (Week 1).

And addiction-habits are immensely powerful. Why? Because all three components (mental, emotional, and physical) have likely been nurtured and strengthened for many years. And habits will fight to the death to stay alive. Therefore, we *must* find a voice stronger than the voice of our insane addiction, which speaks to us sometimes through guile and sometimes with brutal force as it tries to lead us back into the prison of isolation. The good news is that a stronger voice can be found in the power of connection. *Only consistent connection with our Higher Power, ourselves, and trusted others can provide us the reprieve from addiction upon which our lives depend.* Make it personal.

MAKE IT REAL

Review the work you did in Week 4 to remind yourself of the terrible price of addiction. Then list examples of the "insane thinking" you must guard against. Remember that we always get mentally drunk before we get physically drunk. *Mental drunkenness* is another term for insanity, or stinking thinking. What is your "insanity of choice," and how does it most express itself in your life? What mental drunkenness or stinking thinking must you watch out for? Examples include thoughts such as "One drink won't hurt," "Maybe I'm cured and don't know it," "I owe it to myself to see if I can safely use again," "This time it will be different," "I think maybe I was brainwashed in treatment or in my Twelve Step group," and "If I have enough faith, I can use again."

Don't play around with your personal brand of insanity. Alone, we are no match for its power. We simply *must* shine a light on the particular mental drunkenness that we are most vulnerable to. We *must* tell on it. All we are or ever hope to be depends on protecting ourselves from the insanity of addiction.

ACTION STEPS

Of course, no one likes to think of himself or herself as "insane." But living in active addiction is living an insane life. (Similarly, relapse is an act of insanity because it is sentencing yourself to the same misery you once escaped.) Dig deep. Do the work. Call it what it is.

WRITE: (two or three paragraphs, or whatever you can do, on the following topic)

Pick two or three examples of insane "stinking thinking" from this week's reading that you find most familiar. Then give two or three *specific* examples (telling how, when, and in what circumstances) of times you first became aware that you were thinking that way.

SHARE: (with your group or sponsor) several examples of the consequences of allowing these thoughts to remain unchallenged and unchecked in your life.

CONSCIOUS CONTACT: Commit to saying the Third Step aloud on a daily basis: "Made a decision to turn our will and our lives over to the care of God *as we understood Him.*"

• • •

SECTION 4

Moving into the Solution

• WEEK 11 •

Connection Is the Sweet Spot
of Recovery

Why is "keeping it simple" always a good idea? Because something simple always centers on the heart of the matter. It cuts through the clutter and gets to the core—the sweet spot. Think about it: There's a sweet spot in any process you're trying to learn. There's always a central truth that helps all of the pieces make sense, no matter how complex or complicated those individual pieces might be. Once that central truth (sweet spot) is discovered, it's easy to see how everything relates to everything else. In fact, the whole system simply can't exist without that central truth; the process cannot do without it.

So what's the core truth of the God of your understanding—your Higher Power—that's essential to recovery (without which the whole does not exist)? It is *God is love*. If you follow the implications that come from that core truth, every piece of the recovery process makes perfect sense. In the light of that core truth, the connections are recognized, all the pieces are connected, and the map showing the way to the life of the Promises is revealed. That's why the central truth—the sweet spot—of this program is *if isolation is the problem, then connection is the solution*. Just think about this for a while: If spiritual bankruptcy is the problem, and isolation is at the core of spiritual bankruptcy, then the solution must be spiritual living.

So what's at the core of spiritual living? Maintaining our vital connections. Our connection with our Higher Power, self, and another human being *is* the solution. Connection *is* the antidote to relapse.

Connection is the red line on the map of recovery that shows us where the path leads so we won't get lost. Groups, sponsors, meetings, service work, Step classes, working the Steps, becoming honest, open, and willing—these all exist to help us get and stay connected to our Higher Power, self, and others. Every relapse is the result of losing these connections. This book is all about finding ways to connect the dots—all the way from the problem through living the ongoing solution. The only answer to isolation is making our connections with our Higher Power, self, and others *real*.

So what makes these connections real? First, it helps to visualize these connections in the shape of a hoop rather than as three separate entities. Everything in nature is like a hoop, in which everything is connected to everything else. Your connections to your Higher Power, self, and others aren't *experienced* as three different realities. Likewise, although the first three Steps of the Twelve are listed One, Two, and Three, they actually flow into each other and require back and forth movement. Sometimes the focus is on "I can't" (Step One). Sometimes it is on "He can" (Step Two). Sometimes it is on "So I let Him" (Step Three). But in reality, they meld into each other until they're indistinguishable. In thought, they can be separated. In reality (life as it is lived), they are but different facets of the same diamond.

Connection to the God of your understanding is not just about faith; faith is easy. Connection with a loving Higher Power is about trust; trust is what's hard. Trusting that Power is about moving off on a frightening, often difficult path that you know is too dangerous to travel alone. It means there is a Power that cares for you. (That is why the Third Step says we turn our life over to the "care of God." Not to the strength of God or to the power of God, but to the *care* of God.) A saying I heard in the rooms many years ago has always stuck with me: "There will come a time when no power on earth will keep you sober." I'm not sure where it came from, but it seemed to me a simple, elegant way to state a profound truth. Because there *will* come a time when only a rock-solid connection with our Higher Power will keep us sober. This powerful saying means we need to be connected to the God of our understanding, a Power not of this world—a Power that has our back. And when we trust in that Power, facing that time will be no big deal because we know that Power is stronger than anything that can come against us *if only* we "surrender to His will." And our Higher Power's will is only and always for our benefit.

Connection to self is all about rigorous honesty. The Week 10 reading discussed how the insanity of the disease of addiction makes even the most bizarre, crazy ideas seem sensible or even smart. *The slope is slippery.* If left to themselves, addicts can quickly talk themselves into anything—so we must constantly be on guard against self-delusion. "What's real?" must be the watchwords. Sudden urges must be nipped in the bud. The match must be blown out before it lights the fuse that *every time* leads to the box of TNT.

We cannot give ourselves perspective—no person can by himself or herself. That's why a huge part of the solution must be connection to others. And remember that "others" means more than acquaintances, and more than what is usually meant by the word *friends*. The bond that leads to the solution is an amazingly powerful, beautiful reality. It is the experience—not just the thought or the wish or the "wouldn't it be nice," but the *experience* of having special "others," members of your team who will move heaven and earth to come fetch you back into the light when you've wandered into a dark place. It is the *experience* of being totally open and honest with someone whom you know will not throw you away or lock you out. It is the *experience* of being accepted and loved even if your "others" know your deepest, most shameful secrets—just as you accept and love them, no matter what.

Like pleasing incense rising up from these three burning coals, the solution of connecting to our Higher Power, self, and others draws all recovery into itself. Some might ask, "Which is which?" The answer is, "They all are one, each supporting and enhancing the other."

· · ·

Here are two examples of connection that have deeply touched me. The first comes from an e-mail from a woman named Sue, who reached out to Mary, another woman in her group who was foundering in a sea of isolation and loneliness. Mary felt abandoned by every being, both human and divine. "So after group," Sue told her, "we are going to spend some time together." The next day she sent me a follow-up e-mail saying, "We went downtown and had lunch. Then we walked around and looked at the fine homes in that part of town.

After we came back to my house, I washed her car while she took a short nap. Then we cooked dinner and went for a long walk. It was a full day of *fun*."

The second example can only be called a poem. It was written by Michael, a man new to recovery who's finding it hard to believe that the new life opening up for him is possible. Right now he's blinded by the light. But he is standing still and facing the wonder. This is what he wrote:

> When I think, I get visuals. When it's a bad thought, I see what I think is me. I say what I think is me because, before now, I'd never *seen* me. I can't see me with my eyes. It takes *your* eyes for me to see me—providing you love me and are willing to tell me what you see. Sure, I've looked in the mirror and even seen pictures of myself—but that's not me. I need *you* to see me. I know this now because that's how I was able to see me for the first time. The Bible says, "and God said, let us make man in our image" (Genesis 1:26). So now I even know what God looks like! He looks like me when I'm doing the things I'm put on this earth to do—being the man he intended me to be, a loving father, a kind and understanding husband, a loyal friend. Now I know, that's the me God wants to see.

MAKE IT REAL

"It takes your eyes for me to see me" vividly describes the power and importance of connection in recovery. Now it's time to focus on making connection *real* in your life.

ACTION STEPS

Think about *your* connections with your Higher Power, self, and others. How deep are those connections? How honest are they?

WRITE: (two or three paragraphs if you can, on the following topics. Give personal examples.)

1. In my life of addiction, how have I isolated myself from my Higher Power and others?
2. As I look back, what forms of "stinking thinking" led to my last relapse?

SHARE: (with your group or sponsor) some details of your past life that you've never before revealed to anyone.

CONSCIOUS CONTACT: Humbly ask your Higher Power to deepen your ability to trust.

REACH OUT: After a meeting, spend a little time talking to any member who seems shy, fearful, lonely, or sad.

• • •

• WEEK 12 •

I Am the Problem, I Am the Solution

Okay, take a deep breath. Moving into the solution from the work done in Section 2: The Nature of Addiction and Section 3: Getting the Problem Right, is like going from winter to spring. As Week 11 discussed, if the isolation of spiritual bankruptcy is the problem, then moving into the spiritual power of connection is the solution. Why? It is in our connection with our Higher Power, ourselves, and others that we find the joy of living in the solution, of living the Promises.

So far, so good. But what does a life lived in the solution look like? Just what are we talking about? Obviously, there are many, many examples. No one can list them all. The good news is that if we start paying attention, we'll see examples everywhere. The lives of these people in recovery are the dearest, most precious, and most important stories anyone in the human family has to tell. Let me tell you just one of the stories. Some might say one nice little story hardly matters in the grand scheme of things. They might even say this story is unimportant. *But it wasn't unimportant to the men involved.* And the truth is that recovery—the solution—is always a one-on-one, person-to-person, and heart-to-heart kind of thing. It's one person reaching out to another in genuine, nonjudgmental compassion that makes the difference. What comes from the heart touches the heart.

• • •

Ken was one of the "invisible people" in our society, small of stature and almost nonexistent as far as influence goes. He got along by skirting the edges of the crowd and being careful never to draw attention to himself. But that all changed when Ken entered a long-term treat-ment program at a Salvation Army. In this program, everyone works, everyone has a job. After he got his sobriety legs under him, Ken quietly maneuvered to get the job of mopping out the small lobby just inside the facility's front door. Ken did his mopping every day at the same time—when men who were being transferred to the center from various county jails arrived. One of the men in the program with Ken started kidding him about how long it took him to mop the lobby. He even suggested that Ken might be kicked out of the center if he didn't take his job more seriously. Ken assured the man he *did* take his job seriously—but he saw it as a job other than mop-ping. He explained that he wanted his smiling face to be the first face the men from the jails saw when they came in the door. He said he knew how scared and discouraged the men were—because they were just like him when he first arrived. "I want them to know they have family here," Ken said.

MAKE IT REAL

So what does lasting recovery look like? Of what is it made? How does it work?

Look around. Study it. Search out someone whose recovery you admire. Hang around the old-timers. Ask them how they gained their endurance in the program. What did they do to make it for so long? What does your own story tell you? Talk to people at meetings. Ask them to give you specific examples of the difference between "before" and "now" in their lives. What changed for them? How did their personalities change? What is the "secret" of recovery for them?

Our experience tells us that recovery is made of many parts, but that all the parts work to the same end. And that end or purpose is that *I change*. The world doesn't change. It is *I* who has to change. And as I change, my world changes. Just as I am the problem, so I am the solution.

Both the problem and the solution are about *me*. It is in *me*. There was a time when being "the first face the men from the jail see" was the last thing Ken would have wanted. But in recovery he had changed—and you can, too.

After all the asking and listening, all the gathering up of program wisdom you gained from your study, what did you learn? What were the lessons?

1. _____

2. _____

3. _____

4. _____

5. _____

Now compare notes with those who are working through this book with you. What did they learn? What most spoke to their heart? Did anyone tell you they achieved high-level recovery (or any recovery at all) by isolating? By going it alone? Did any of them experience growth in a vacuum? How important were the connections they'd made? What does that tell you? Whatever you came up with—*that* is the solution. You are looking at it. That is what all the fuss and fury, all the work and effort, all the struggle into the sunlight of recovery is about. Working a program of recovery—and recovery itself—is not a theory, and it is not a philosophy. It is a way of life that produces specific results for those who diligently apply themselves to its principles. What changes is the way I live. What changes is me.

ACTION STEPS

How often we blame our lack of progress on exterior circumstances! We see our problems as someone else's fault or just plain bad luck. Until we identify the *real* problem, our "bad luck" can only continue. To find both the problem and the solution, look in the mirror—and do the suggested work.

WRITE: (two or three paragraphs if you can, on the following topics. Give personal examples.)
1. Many of us fantasize about winning the lottery, assuming it would solve all our problems. In the light of your current situation, describe your root problem that has nothing to do with money.
2. Read the Third Step prayer in the Big Book. Explain the meaning of "Relieve me of the burden of self."

SHARE: (with your group or sponsor)
1. At least one specific behavior you can practice to avoid isolation.
2. Your understanding of why working the Steps is "the engine of your spiritual awakening."

REACH OUT: Ask old-timers in the program to sit down with you over a cup of coffee and reveal some of their "sobriety secrets."

• • •

• WEEK 13 •

The First Step Is Free

If it is clear enough, a diagram can help explain a concept. This simple diagram has been used with thousands of recovering people to help them visualize what it takes to move into the solution of recovery.

Imagine that the diagram is an actual goalpost with a line drawn down the middle of the uprights. The left side of the goalpost says ALCOHOLIC/ADDICTIVE THINKING, and the right says RECOVERY/SPIRITUAL THINKING. A large X stands in the middle of the left-hand side of the goalpost.

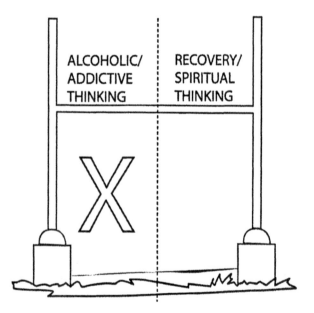

Pretty simple, isn't it?

A person in active addiction is stuck/pinned/nailed/riveted in the middle of the insanity that active addiction is (Week 10). There is a consequence—a terrible cost—of being stuck on that side of the line (Week 4). The cost? It's everything that matters most to us. As a sponsor of mine says, "Addiction doesn't *take* anything from us. We throw it away." Either way, we lose. And so does everyone who cares for us.

Looking at the diagram, the solution to the problem seems obvious enough. If you no longer want to pay the heavy cost of an active addiction, *move across the line.* Move from the left side of the goalpost to the right side. And then, once delivered, stay there! It sounds easy enough, but what does it take to make that happen?

Addictions are incredibly strong (weeks 5, 9, and 10). How can we possibly leap from the left-hand side to the right? The answer is, "*We* don't do it." We alone aren't strong enough. We need help. Once again, let's reflect on the saying "There will come a time when no power on earth will keep us sober." A time like that sounds pretty grim—unless we find *someone or something to do for us what we can't do for ourselves.* The good news is that there is a power not of this earth that promises to deliver us *if* that power were sought. And the first step of that deliverance is *free.*

What I'm talking about is the endlessly mysterious *spiritual experience.* I say "mysterious" because every spiritual awakening is unique. These awakenings occur differently for different people. They may come with a pounce or a crawl. We humans cannot cause them—not for ourselves and surely not for anyone else. We can create an environment where they are most likely to happen, but we cannot cause them. Some people call these experiences "hitting bottom," "kissing concrete," "a moment of clarity," "a tap on the shoulder," "a coming to consciousness," or "when enough is finally enough." Spiritual experiences have lots of names, but the names all tell the same story. As we read in chapter 5 of the Big Book, "Our personal adventures before and after make clear three pertinent ideas:

- That we were alcoholic and could not manage our own lives.
- That probably no human power could relieve our alcoholism.
- That God could and would if he were sought."

Look again at the diagram of the goalposts. Then envision how those three "pertinent ideas" play out: God picks us up (at X) and deposits us on the right side of the dividing line. We don't *earn* that free ride. Sometimes we haven't even asked for it. And we don't get the ride because we are so smart or good or favored over others. No one knows—or ever will know—why some seem to "get it" and some don't. What is clear is that we are picked up and brought into the light. How did that happen for you? What was your First Step experience like? When was "enough finally enough" for you? Was it a surprise? Were you seeking help? Who was there? What happened? Here is where the solution starts: Our Higher Power steps in and picks us up like the wounded children that we are and says, "Where you are is too dangerous. Come away. Come with me and stand over here. We will move away from all your tears and suffering." There is no solution—not in the Twelve Step way of doing things— without a surrender of our power into the care of a loving God of our understanding.

Some have problems with the thought of surrendering to a loving God, or Higher Power. Why? Perhaps they confuse "God" with their negative experiences with religion, church, or a specific school of theology. Often, we have trouble accepting a loving God who stands ready to help us as soon as we ask because of the guilt, shame, and self-contempt we picked up during active addiction. (Although it's more likely the guilt, shame, and self-contempt were already in place long before the addiction ever started.) Such walls of self-hatred, guilt, and shame make acceptance of any gift impossible.

By the same token, faith is easy. It's trust that is hard. Loving is easy. Accepting that *we* are loved is what defeats many of us. Helping others is nearly always much easier than asking for help for ourselves. Whatever the "spiritual condition" we bring to our recovery, living in the solution requires a deep and honest connection with the God of our understanding, the Power greater than ourselves. This is a relationship many of us fear and shy away from. Some of us have been running from this connection our whole lives. But the heart cannot be outrun. Those who surrender discover that what most frightened them was also what they most sought. *Stand still.* Over the years, I have seen countless individuals run from God and the spirituality of the program. They struggle with the very idea of spirituality. Above all, they seem to fear connection. Instead of simply standing still and allowing themselves to be embraced, they substitute nonstop service work, twice-a-day meetings, or memorization of the Big Book. These are all laudable activities, but there is *no* substitute for deliberately and humbly connecting with the God of our understanding.

Perhaps you are one such person. Have you tried (or are trying) to substitute doing for being? Or talking for listening? Or show over substance? Maybe you have never, like Ken in the Week 12 reading, "mopped out the lobby" just so you could be the first smiling face seen by a sick, broken, terrified brother or sister who comes among us seeking the solution. If so, I urge you to just *stand still*. Listen and become teachable. *Seek.* Our Eleventh Step says, "We sought through prayer and meditation." *Sought* means we went looking for. And prayer is mostly about listening, not talking or saying words. It's about listening to the one who calls us out of our self-destructive addiction.

Make a list. It's strange how many of us willingly tell the worst moments of our addiction to anyone who will listen, but hesitate to share our spiritual journey. Many find it profoundly embarrassing. On the whole, far more drunkalogs are heard in the rooms than stories of spiritual awakenings. Why do you suppose that is? Why glory in the problem when the solution is so much more interesting—to say nothing of *important*? Moving into the solution is moving into one's spirituality. Our Twelfth Step says, "Having had a spiritual awakening as the result of these steps. . . ." Think about it. Working the Steps is the engine of your spiritual awakening, which is at the heart of the solution. Why? Because spiritual bankruptcy (Week 9) is at the heart of the problem.

MAKE IT REAL

What have *you* "awakened to"? What have been your spiritual experiences, starting with the first free experience that took you from addictive thinking to spiritual thinking, to living in the solution? What moments of clarity have you experienced? *We see what we pay attention to.* So let's pay attention to the wonders and the changes that are happening in us. *Stand still. Stop. Reflect. Think.* Meet yourself in the inner court of your own soul. Look deeply into the mirror of self and record what you see. How did it all start for you? What experience rescued you from the depths of hopelessness and put you down on safe land? List your spiritual awakenings. Share them with others. Then listen to their stories as well. Receive the wisdom and the wonder that has been ushered into their lives.

ACTION STEPS

It seems hard to believe that the gift of recovery was always there, waiting for us to come and get it. What prevents us from accepting the loving support that's so willingly offered? Do the work suggested and begin to work your way out of spiritual bankruptcy.

WRITE: (two or three paragraphs if you can, on the following topics. Give personal examples.)
1. What was the "moment of clarity" that started you out on your spiritual journey? What insight first penetrated the dark fog of addiction?
2. Explain why "working the Steps is the engine of spiritual awakening."

SHARE: (with your group or sponsor) examples of the times you've substituted "show for substance" and how that resulted in self-contempt.

CONSCIOUS CONTACT: Thank God for lifesaving "second chances."

PRACTICE: Pay attention to the small, steady changes being made in your habitual thoughts and feelings.

• • •

• WEEK 14 •

Earning the Solution
by Working the Solution

Are you doing a quick run-through of the weeks to see how all the dots connect? If so, fine. But when you're ready to dig in, please don't skip the work in *any* of the weeks. Each preceding week is a foundation block for the next week to build on. As with everything else in this world, we get out of an endeavor just about as much as we put into it. Little in, little out. What we are dealing with here is *far too important* for anything but maximum effort—and the rewards we will receive from this work are truly immense.

Go back to Week 13 and look at the diagram of the goalpost. Remember that the first movement from the left side of active addiction to the right side of recovery is a gift. It is free. We are simply picked up and dropped in the middle of a "moment of clarity." The veil parts and we see a new light. Why then? Why not ten years earlier or five years later? Who knows? It's a gift of grace. And the only appropriate response to a gift is to humbly accept it and be grateful. But this movement is only the first step. *The goal is not just to reach the right side of the goalpost, it is to hang on—and continue to move on into the life of the Promises.*

The second step of the recovery process must be earned—which means we have to work the solution. When our inner eye opens after that first gift of grace (whether that was a blinding white light experience or the more common step-by-step "educational variety" of spiritual experience), we are still the same person. We *see* more, but we are not more. The habits of character that constitute spiritual bankruptcy are still there, still in us. Dealing with those negative mental and behavioral habits is the work left to be done. The program has many names for that work, including "improving our conscious contact with God," "working the Steps," "going to meetings," "getting and using a sponsor," "studying the Big Book," "practicing an attitude of gratitude," and "always, always being of service to others." Other actions could be listed, but all lists include these. All these behaviors are right, good, and necessary. *They work if we work.* No one put it better or more simply than AA's cofounder Dr. Bob when he counseled: *Trust God, help others, and clean house.*

Certainly, I strongly encourage all these activities. But rather than going into greater detail on any one of these important endeavors, my purpose is to "lift the lid" on or reveal what is happening inside us as we're doing this work. The point is that *we* are changing (Week 12)—even when we don't notice the change, even when we suspect that we're missing the boat because others seem to be changing so much more and so much faster than we are. But change *is* happening—on a level far beneath and beyond what we're able to perceive. New foundation stones of our character and personality are gradually sliding into place. We are beginning to enter and embrace the world with new and different values.

In Week 9, we focused on the values that underlie our problem of spiritual bankruptcy. Our deepest beliefs are behind all of our thoughts, feelings, and actions. Because values live at the core of our beliefs, these values change as our beliefs change. And as our beliefs change, *we* change. Recovery is the process of internalizing and acting on very different values than those we embraced during active addiction. As we launch into recovery by taking recovery actions, our values begin to change—though not always easily. Some of our old fears and attachments are so entrenched that they leave claw marks on our spirits as they are nudged out of the way. But change *does* happen if we keep pressing on.

Every recovery action is a practice session of a new value. Recovery is the internalization of new values. Listed below are ten such new values. Rather than artificially lining up one value with one recovery action (which is neat and tidy, like listing the first three Steps in a neat, orderly progression when they work differently in real life), I'd like you to ask yourself which recovery behavior (working the Steps, reading the Big Book, practicing deeper conscious contact with the God of your understanding, and so on) *you* think lines up with each specific value. How do *you* best learn and practice the listed value? Or identify a specific value you've seen acted out in someone else's story. Where have you seen this value in action? How might you consciously, intentionally act out this value now—whereas in your using days, you wouldn't even have thought of such an action? Play with this task. Work with it. Lift the lid on all the recovery behaviors and reveal what is happening inside. This task is like opening the back of a watch to see all the wondrous spinning wheels and cogs that work together to keep the correct time. Here are the ten new values:

1. ENDURANCE: exercising discipline, not quitting, pressing on.
2. HONESTY: facing the truth, telling the truth, acting the truth.
3. PATIENCE: accepting that things happen in their own time, not yours.
4. CARING: allowing others to matter, resolving to make a difference.
5. FORGIVENESS: being at peace with imperfection in self and others.
6. HUMILITY: accepting that everything is not about you.
7. TEACHABILITY: opening your mind to learning something new.
8. RESPONSIBILITY: stop blaming and evading; if you spill the milk, you clean it up.
9. GENEROSITY: opening your hand and heart to bring new blessings to others.
10. COURAGE: facing your challenges whether or not you *feel* brave.

This is a gigantic sandbox to play in. Have fun.

MAKE IT REAL

The success of any program is not in what is taught, but in what is learned. *The best way to learn is to teach.* Why? Because what we can't clearly explain, we don't really know. If at all possible, spend time talking with members of your group. Teach, explain, and give examples of how recovery works from your life and others' lives. Explain the connection between the problem and the solution as outlined in these pages. Using the diagram of the goalposts, describe (because it can't really be explained; spirit is as spirit does) the first step of moving from active addiction to recovery. Tell about your First Step experience, how and when you were picked up and taken from the left side of the goalpost to the right side of recovery. Reflect on your own story and explain to those around you how recovery must be earned and how it must be worked. But also give examples of how a miracle gained can also be lost. Explain relapse. Explain how our twenty-four-hour reprieve is won, day by day. Report to yourself and someone else the evidence of how values are shifting in your daily life.

Now, pat yourself on the back and give a huge shout of gratitude to God for having made it this far in your recovery. As our grandkids say, "You're a rock star!"

ACTION STEPS

As your work commences, remember that we're only taking *one day at a time.* Can you "do one right thing" and follow that with another one *just for today?* Don't let self-doubt stop you before you even get started. Each twenty-four hours is another rung up on the climb out of spiritual bankruptcy.

WRITE: (two or three paragraphs if you can, on the following topics. Give personal examples.)
  1. Describe two of the negative values that supported your life of addiction.
  2. Choose two positive values from the list on page 65. Suggest a few behaviors that could make these values real in your life.

SHARE: (with your group or sponsor) your understanding of the saying "The program works if you work it."

CONSCIOUS CONTACT: Practice trust. Ask your Higher Power's help in overcoming dangerous mental and behavioral habits.

REACH OUT: Find a friend in the group who also feels daunted by the amount of work to be done. Make a pact to move on together, supporting each other.

• • •

• WEEK 15 •

The Life of the Promises

The work in weeks 4 through 10 (Section 2: The Nature of Addiction and Section 3: Getting the Problem Right) can seem like an awesome burden. But addiction itself is an awesome burden, isn't it? It's critical that a person in recovery—again, especially in that first all-important year—clearly understands the true nature of the task, the work that lies ahead. In this case, ignorance is definitely not bliss. For those dealing with addiction to alcohol and/or drugs, whether dually diagnosed or not, ignorance can kill. (For proof, simply call to mind someone you know whose addiction proved fatal.)

But there's more to the story than just struggling to protect yourself from the beast of addiction. There is more to your story than your drunkalogs. After a while, drunkalogs get boring. The real story of recovery is in the bounce—first hitting bottom and then "bouncing" up to a life in recovery that is better than you ever could have imagined. That story, the story of living in the solution, is never boring.

Realizing that you've hit bottom is a significant achievement. Getting to a first birthday is a significant achievement. But *every day* of a spiritual, recovering life is a gift beyond measure. Think of a seesaw. Imagine that one end is held down by the weight of the "nature of addiction." It's *heavy*; the weight of addiction is no joke. But then visualize the weight of the "nature of recovery" coming down on the other side.

As far as addiction takes people down, so high does recovery lift them up. The deepest scarlet of guilt, shame, rage, fear, and isolation the addict has experienced can give way to the shining white of forgiveness, compassion, understanding, and nonjudgmental acceptance of others. Crushing isolation will be replaced with connection and a fierce commitment to find those still suffering so you can usher them into the blessed light that recovery offers all who would accept its gift. Simply put, recovery—also called living in the Promises—is worth a thousand times the effort it takes to claim a seat by the flame that is spiritual living.

The rewards of spiritual living are indeed many. Read this e-mail that Sara sent to her group upon returning home after cancer surgery: "I'm sharing this with all of you because there's nothing quite so moving as discovering that one is not alone. And also, if I didn't tell you the truth about my situation, you wouldn't have known to pray for me. The strength of our group is so wonderful! No matter what the outcome will be, I know that I will always be loved and cared for by my very dear friends in our Saturday Morning Group."

And here's an excerpt from an inmate's letter, sharing that he got back into recovery in prison:

> There's a kid in here named Jerry. He was convicted on a drug charge and has a couple more years to do. He looks like he's about twelve. He gets messed with pretty bad in here. One day I asked him if it would be okay if we talked. He was so happy I thought he was going to cry. He said his family had thrown him away, and he was all alone. I told him he wasn't all alone anymore because I wanted to be his friend. I remembered how important it was to me when I first got into recovery that someone thought I was worthy of friendship. Well, after about a week of hanging around with Jerry, everyone stopped messing with him. One of the real hard cases in here came up to me and asked if I knew Jerry from the streets. When I told him no, he sat down and started talking with me. His name is Bob. Now all three of us go to AA meetings every week—and Bob isn't acting so tough anymore.

Here are some more stories from local AA groups that speak of the new life available to us all.

• • •

The grizzled old man looked like a hunk of rock wrapped in old leather. He'd been in the group as long as anyone could remember. Today he was patiently listening to a new, young member of the group who was still in treatment. The kid was complaining about all the "stupid rules" he had to obey in the center. The old man let him say his piece before quietly advising, "Keeping rules, stupid or not, won't keep you sober. What *can* keep you sober is your *willingness* to keep the rules—whether you think they're stupid or not." For a long moment, no one said a thing. True wisdom often leaves silence in its wake.

• • •

George felt called to start a late-night AA meeting, after the third-shift workers at a nearby factory went off the clock. For two years, no one showed up. But George was always there, Big Book in hand, ready for a meeting. That was years ago. These days, dozens of men and women attend that meeting. Recently, George was asked if he ever felt like a failure during those first two years. His answer was "No. The only failure would be if someone needed a meeting and I wasn't there."

• • •

Ginny, who is old and overweight, is the dedicated voice at the end of the phone in her small community. When a suffering alcoholic calls for help, Ginny always answers. She spends so much time on the phone that large, ugly bruises sometimes develop on her arms where she leans on the table while talking. "So," she says, "a couple of the boys made me a sheepskin pad to lean on. They take good care of this old lady." Everyone loves Ginny, and they're ready to respond, day or night, when she calls them to go out and "help one of us who is lost find the way back home." At one time, Ginny had been in her own dark alley, and she never forgot how that felt. Now she says she is just repaying the debt she incurred when someone went out and got her. Her favorite program saying is "Program isn't a gift. It's a debt." A fierce fire burns behind this sweet old lady's eyes when she tells anyone who will listen, "Someone came and got you, and by God, you'd better be willing to go get those who are still suffering."

• • •

Dick struggled with sobriety for nearly fifty years. (Some of our number struggle more than others. It is not for us to judge why this is so. We do not live in anyone else's skin, so how would we know the intensity of their battle?) Dick may have relapsed a thousand times, but he got up a thousand and one. After each relapse, he was the first one to show up for his 6:00 a.m. meeting. No matter how shamed, humiliated, or defeated Dick felt, he always got up and tried again. He was drinking coffee after one of his "start-over meetings" at a nearby coffee shop when another chronic relapser spotted him and made a beeline over to his table. The man made a huge show of happiness and gratitude at seeing his friend Dick back among the living. He didn't care what anyone around them thought or said. He was on to something far more important than such trivial matters. He asked Dick to be his sponsor. Dick declined. He couldn't understand why anyone would want a sponsor who had such a hard time staying sober himself. But his friend said that was just the point. "I can't relate to someone ten or twenty years clean. I need someone who struggles like I do. I need a sponsor with the courage not to quit. That's you," he said. "You're just who I need. Besides," he continued, "maybe we can help keep each other standing up longer than we have before." And so the two of them walked onward together, leaning on each other.

MAKE IT REAL

It is by such heroic attitudes and actions, and only by such attitudes and actions, that this sorry old world may be saved. *If you want what we have, do what we do.* And welcome to the greatest club on God's green earth. Often, a person in recovery is growing without even knowing it. Most of us are terrible judges of who we are or how we are doing, which is why we desperately need the perspective of others (Week 14). Often, people move into the life of the Promises without ever noticing they've changed their address. Growth is most often gradual.

In the Action Steps, you'll take a closer look at your life through the lens of the Promises. Following, as a reminder, is a list of those Promises as found in the Big Book.

1. We are going to know a new freedom and a new happiness.
2. We will not regret the past nor wish to shut the door on it.
3. We will comprehend the word serenity.
4. We will know peace.
5. No matter how far down the scale we have gone, we will see how our experience can benefit others.
6. That feeling of uselessness and self-pity will disappear.
7. We will lose interest in selfish things and gain interest in our fellows.
8. Self-seeking will slip away.
9. Our whole attitude and outlook upon life will change.
10. Fear of people and of economic insecurity will leave us.
11. We will intuitively know how to handle situations which used to baffle us.
12. We will suddenly realize that our Higher Power is doing for us what we could not do for ourselves.

ACTION STEPS

Okay. Now we know that the recovery road is a long uphill slog. But the good news is that it's doable. And the even better news is that the rewards are beyond imagining.

WRITE: (two or three paragraphs if you can, on the following topics. Give personal examples.)

1. Write about two of the Promises that seem most desirable to you. Explain why.
2. As best you can, explain your understanding of "the life of the Promises."

SHARE: (with your group or sponsor) when and how you recently sought the help of your Higher Power.

REACH OUT: Identify someone whose long-term recovery you admire. Ask that person to share with you his or her experience with "the life of the Promises."

SECTION 5

Attitude Adjustment Required

• WEEK 16 •

Honesty: Secrets Kill

Values practiced long enough become attitudes. Our attitudes, then, are expressed values—the eyes through which we view the world. You might say that our attitudes are the "inner dictionaries" we use to interpret and find meaning in the way we live. It doesn't take any great intellectual leap to realize (especially if you've done the work in weeks 9 and 14) that a recovering person's attitudes are far different than the attitudes of an active addict. Recovery *requires* an attitude adjustment—and delivers it as the result of staying connected. As our values and attitudes change, *we* change. And that ongoing process of change (Week 12) is the solution.

The next five weeks dig a little deeper into five key attitudes that promote growth in the fertile ground of recovery. The first attitude is honesty.

In both the Big Book and the Twelve and Twelve, the founders repeatedly stated that recovery is far more than physical sobriety. They defined our "problem" (whether or not magnified through the lens of a dual diagnosis) as *spiritual bankruptcy*. Let's be clear about that. "Our problem" is not the substance. "Our problem" is the person using the substance—us.

As envisioned by the founders, the solution to our problem is a *transformation of character*—in effect, a realignment of personality. Central to that transformation is the bedrock of rigorous honesty. Why? It is only on that rock that the fortress of recovery can be built. Dishonesty in any of its many forms is the wedge that pries open the door to personal disaster.

At this point in your journey, the simple yet critical question is "What are you *not* sharing? What carryovers of your addictive thinking or behavior are you not 'telling on'?"

The slippery slope toward relapse always begins with some form of dishonesty. It may be a rationalization or an example of "stinking thinking" entertained too long. It may be a minimization of something that isn't minimal at all. Often, it's a recurring thought or urge that for various reasons we're not willing to put on the table. Perhaps it is hidden away because of guilt or shame or fear that "If I told anyone about this, I could be put in prison—or at the very least I'd be kicked out of my group." We convince ourselves, "No one else in the civilized world has thoughts like this. I must be sicker than anyone who ever got into recovery." And so the offending thought is hidden in the dark—where it becomes toxic.

Relapse almost always happens that way. It's a process. The slide starts with an untold thought, an unshared urge, a persistent whisper in the mind. Hidden from the healing light of fellowship, like mushrooms in the dark, the dangerous thoughts and feelings flourish and pick up steam. In the person's sickening and distorted mind, the most bizarre thoughts start to seem sensible. Before long, they escalate from "probably making sense" to seeming "absolutely true." After that, it's too late.

Whoever first said, "An alcoholic by himself or herself is in bad company," should have their handprints etched in the walk of fame in front of Grauman's Chinese Theater. Same with whoever first said, "Our own self-talk always seems to make sense, no matter how crazy it is." Or consider the saying many of us are most familiar with: "We're only as sick as our secrets."

No one is saying that honesty is easy, especially *rigorous* honesty. Talk to the old-timers—those who have stood the test of time—about the role of honesty in long-standing recovery; there the story and the truth is told. Check with those whose recovery you admire. What do they have to say about honesty? *The flat-out truth is that there is no recovery without honesty.*

Here is a short list of topics that people new—or not so new—to recovery often keep secrets about. If the topic that gives you the most trouble with honesty has been left out, write it in the space provided.

Be aware that it is right here, at the tipping point between honesty and keeping secrets, that the beast of addiction and relapse is pounding on your door. Ask yourself if you've been honest about all of these topics and shared your truth with someone in the Fellowship.

1. Urges and stinking thinking such as "Maybe I can use again" or "Maybe I'm cured" or "No one will ever know" (any insane thought of using again)
2. Escalating and deepening depressive thoughts; perhaps even thoughts of ending your life
3. Any troubling issues around sexual activity or sexual issues
4. Any troubling issues around finances
5. Any troubling issues around relationships
6. Increasing urges to get back into "the life" on the streets
7. Any vexing problems that arise around family, jobs, stressful situations, anger, and rage—or any situation that would "pull you off your recovery square"
8. Urges to isolate, break connections to recovery fellowship, make excuses for "not showing up"
9. Increasing feelings of self-contempt, unworthiness, and low self-esteem
10. Or _____

Remember, we aren't expected to share our hidden thoughts and vulnerabilities with everyone. Not everyone is trustworthy. The point is that we need to share these thoughts with *someone*. We *must* learn to trust if we are to move out of spiritual bankruptcy. Don't trust everyone, but do trust someone.

MAKE IT REAL

Suppose you are grading yourself at this point in recovery on "rigorous honesty with someone." What score between 1 and 10 (10 being high) would you give yourself? Some aspects of recovery are more important than others. As far as ongoing recovery is concerned, honesty is as important as it gets.

A C T I O N   S T E P S

Through long practice, most of us become quite adept at dodging and weaving around the unvarnished truth. If the issues are too painful or shameful, we may not even tell ourselves the truth. Now is the time to face up to that failure. It's true that the truth hurts—but it also sets us free.

WRITE: (two or three paragraphs if you can, on the following topics. Give personal examples.)
1. Explain the difference between "cash register honesty" and the rigorous honesty with self and others required for recovery.
2. Give personal examples of dishonesty regarding two topics on the list.

SHARE: (with your group or sponsor)
1. Tell about a time in your life when you minimized something that was not at all minimal.
2. Reveal a secret you've never been willing to share before.

CONSCIOUS CONTACT: Ask your Higher Power to lead you to those in the Fellowship who can be most helpful to you.

REACH OUT: Have you asked someone to be your sponsor yet? Look for an old-timer whose sharing never seems to be "sugar-coated."

• • •

• WEEK 17 •

Gratitude

Gratitude is the second attitude that we can't do without. The Big Book tells us that resentments are the number one source of relapse. *Gratitude is the opposite of resentment.* Gratitude is about counting blessings rather than complaints and grudges. A person who regularly practices an attitude of gratitude will not relapse.

- An attitude of gratitude anchors a person on the right side of the goalpost of recovery.
- An attitude of gratitude is where all the pieces of recovery come together.
- An attitude of gratitude is the result of consistently staying connected to our Higher Power, self, and trusted others.
- An attitude of gratitude is at the heart of the spiritual condition that provides the twenty-four-hour reprieve from active addiction.
- An attitude of gratitude is the yellow brick road leading to the Promises.

A sure sign that someone is wandering off his or her recovery path and heading for relapse is increased negativity, complaining, and whining. A friend and counselor recently told about driving a carful of men in early recovery to a meeting. He said that two of the men were doing fine, but he could tell that the third fellow was just about out the door. Then he added, "All the man did was complain all night about the program he was in. He went on and on about the rules—he was even griping about having to go to meetings." Later we learned the counselor was right. That man left the program within the week.

Review the values involved in spiritual bankruptcy (Week 9): *ego, instant gratification, overemphasis on feelings, dishonesty,* and *total reliance on self.* It's easy to see that living these values leaves no room for gratitude. It's impossible to grow gratitude from such stony ground.

Conversely, think about the ten values outlined in Week 14 (Earning the Solution by Working the Solution): *endurance, honesty, patience, caring, forgiveness, humility, teachability, responsibility, generosity,* and *courage.* All of these values lead to an attitude of gratitude. The fruit of these positive values opens us to recognizing the blessings in our lives.

CONNECT THE DOTS

Explain the following in your own words. Use as many specific, personal experiences as you can to back up your remarks.

1. What is the problem? Why is it called spiritual bankruptcy?
2. What is the solution? What is meant by "living the spirituality of the program"?
3. How does living the spirituality of the program always lead to the attitude of gratitude?

WHY ME?

Someone who hasn't practiced the attitude of gratitude is often heard grumbling, "Why me? Why do such terrible things happen to *me?* Why do I have such bad luck? Why do I have to do work that others don't? Why can't I drink like normal people? Why do I have to come from the family I do?"

Whiners never run out of things to whine about. But there is another version of "Why me?" that has to do with all the blessings we have been given—and are still being given. Why are we so blessed? Why have we been given this chance to recover? Why are we lucky enough to be born at a time in history when such help is available? Why are we so fortunate to be offered the kind of fellowship most of the rest of the world doesn't even know exists?

Those engaged in recognizing, accepting, and celebrating their good fortune never run out of reasons for gratitude.

Think of the face of a clock. If the history of the human race is represented by the twelve hours on the clock's face—and it is understood that alcoholism and addiction have been savaging humans that entire time, and it has only been since 1935 that an organized, effective method of dealing with addiction has existed—then how blessed and fortunate are we who were born in those few seconds of the clock's twelve hours in which there is an answer to alcoholism and addiction!

Why me? Why us?

It's likely you know one or more people who came before you who died of alcoholism or another addiction. Perhaps it was a parent or grandparent. They were not given a chance to join the Fellowship. There were no "rooms" for them. They were simply unfortunate to have been born before the program existed or was widely known or available. Their necks were bared to the wolf, and there was nothing they could do about it.

Why me? Why us? Why were we so blessed? Why are we so lucky?

Who knows? But the gift was given to us. We had best not squander a treasure so freely given.

MAKE IT REAL

In all things, we become what we practice. This holds true with the central recovery practice of gratitude. It's simple: Every day, list three blessings you are aware of; keep these lists and read them at the end of each week to see how blessed your life is. On the eighth day, start a new list.

As one man said, "I'm thankful for being alive today. I could have been dead a hundred times."

A recovering woman who had recently lost her father to alcoholism said, "I'm grateful for the gift of hitting bottom. I don't think my father ever did. He never had a thought about quitting as far as I know. But I am given a chance!"

Once again, don't fail to do the writing. Do the work. Don't just read this exercise and dismiss it with, "Yeah, it's a good idea. I'll have to try that sometime." Now is the time! Making a practice of logging your recognized blessings may even turn out to be the extra effort that saves your life.

ACTION STEPS

We human beings are very quick to take our good fortune for granted. While some 50,000 people a day die of starvation in this world, we grumble and complain when everything doesn't go our way. Narrow self-interest blinds us to the many blessings that surround us. That's why *paying attention* is absolutely necessary to growing gratitude.

WRITE: (two or three paragraphs if you can, on the following topics. Give personal examples.)
1. List two or three of your habitual resentments. Explain why you think each one is rational or irrational.
2. On a scale of 1 to 10, rate how well you recognize and show appreciation for your blessings. Give examples.

SHARE: (with your group or sponsor)
1. Talk about two or three people or circumstances for which you are truly grateful. Explain why each one is valuable to you.
2. Describe something you habitually grumble or whine about (either in your own mind or out loud to others).

CONSCIOUS CONTACT: Thank your Higher Power for the gift of the Twelve Step program.

REACH OUT: Get in touch with someone who has been consistently loyal and encouraging to you. Acknowledge that person's contribution to your life.

• • •

• WEEK 18 •

Endurance

Of all possible attitudes, why choose to focus on endurance?

The answer is that recovery is a marathon, not a sprint. Even though we can only arrest our addiction on a daily basis, the goal is to invoke that reprieve every twenty-four hours for as long as we live. And that takes endurance. It takes the mentality of a long-distance runner.

At first, endurance might seem to be a homely attitude (especially in our "it's all about me" culture), but there are many times in lifelong recovery when only the dogged toughness of endurance will pull a person through.

We human beings really love the big *wow.* We are thrilled by the ninety-eight-yard touchdown run of a superb athlete, and rightly so. But what almost always goes unremarked is the role of the lineman who opened the hole (and may well have taken a good wallop to his head in doing so) that made the dramatic run possible. Then, when it is time to go on the offensive again, that same mud-smeared line-man steps back onto the field, opening holes and turning back rampaging linebackers who rush the passer no matter what it costs.

That's *endurance*—doing the hard work again and again despite the costs. In recovery, of course, there is always this added dimension: No matter what it costs, it isn't half as much as the price we will pay if we *don't* endure (Week 4).

In truth, the best recovery book is depicted in the lives of people working out their daily bread in the Fellowship. The true miracle of recovery is best seen in the glory of *your* story. *Recovery is not a spectator sport. It is totally about participation.*

That's why this week begins with a story that illustrates and high-lights the importance and glory of endurance.

• • •

Jimmy R. lived in Minnesota and was a heroic member of the Fellowship. When he passed at age ninety-three, he had fifty-four years in AA. He went back so far that he and Dr. Bob used to fish together. One of his prized possessions, in fact, was a photograph of Dr. Bob and himself holding up a long stringer of fish.

The last dozen or so years of Jimmy's life were spent in chronic deep pain as a result of shingles. During many of those years, the pain kept Jimmy from regularly attending his beloved Friday night meeting. But his friend Dwayne—a fellow member in his eighties with "only" thirty-seven years in the program and who needed to pull an oxygen tank behind him—called Jimmy every Friday morning to see if he was well enough to make that evening's meeting. Jimmy never stopped getting a chuckle out of telling Dwayne, "Thirty-seven years, huh? You got a good start there, young fella. Just keep on keeping on!"

One cold, blustery Friday in March, Dwayne made his usual call. The pain was manageable that day, Jimmy said. He figured he could make the meeting that evening.

So there they were, two old men, one pulling an oxygen tank and the other leaning on his friend to help ease the pain, heading out the door in miserable weather, going to their meeting. It would take more than bad weather, a heavy oxygen tank, and pain that was "manageable" to keep them from making their meeting.

When the old fellows got seated, someone asked, "Why go to so much effort, Jimmy? Why would you work so hard just to get to a meeting? Surely you don't get thirsty anymore."

Jimmy's answer came right from the heart of the heart of all that is best in the program. With a twinkle in his eye, he said, "Oh, no. It's not about me. It's about the new man. Maybe there's someone here who's just starting off, someone I can help."

• • •

I know that is how it happened because I was the one who asked him why he went to so much trouble to get to his meeting.

Our best lessons come from the old-timers who have kept their heads and hearts in the program. They got to be old-timers by living the virtue (virtues are baptized values) of endurance. They lived it so long and practiced it so consistently that the virtue turned into an attitude. And that attitude became the square they stood on, no matter what. No matter if practicing their program was sometimes inconvenient, whether they felt like it or not, whether they were in pain or not, whether or not they "had a good start" of thirty-seven years or were true old-timers who'd gone fishing with Dr. Bob.

You can find these people if you look for them. Sit in their shadow. Listen to them. Watch how they live. See how they act and react to all that life throws at them. Look beneath the surface appearance of "where they are now" and see what values, virtues, and attitudes have fueled their lives. See for yourself how the quality of endurance helped them make it to this point.

MAKE IT REAL

Reflect on the three dimensions of staying connected to your Higher Power, self, and trusted others (Week 11). Are your connections enduring? Have there been any slips? Does your program need to tighten up, toughen up, and endure another day longer in rigorous connectedness?

HIGHER POWER: Surrender, connection, communication. How goes it with your conscious connection to the God of your understanding?

SELF: No little lies, no sinking into stinking thinking, no truce with your addiction. How goes your rigorous honesty with self?

TRUSTED OTHERS: Taking a risk, telling the absolute truth, showing up, and standing up for others in recovery. How goes it with staying connected to others?

A C T I O N   S T E P S

Endurance takes preparation. At the beginning of a race, it isn't hard to run a few fast laps. But a weak, out-of-shape runner simply isn't able to complete a marathon. That's why the program must be practiced daily. Lifelong sobriety means being willing and able to keep going, rain or shine.

WRITE: (two or three paragraphs if you can, on the following topics. Give personal examples.)
1. Give a short account of your track record in pursuing long-term goals.
2. List three ways you could prepare yourself to keep going for the long haul.

SHARE: (with your group or sponsor) examples of stinking thinking that have halted your progress in the past.

CONSCIOUS CONTACT: Turn your life and your will over to the care of your Higher Power three times a day.

REACH OUT: Find a "workout buddy" in your group; pledge mutual support and encouragement.

• • •

• WEEK 19 •

Teachability

Our only hope in keeping our addiction arrested lies in our spirituality. That's what sobriety and ongoing recovery are conditioned on. And a key component of that healthy spiritual condition is openness to learning. It is about being teachable.

What did you learn today? Was it something you'd never thought of before? Or was it something you already knew, but, because you were now more open, you were able to understand on a different and deeper level?

We can exhaust ourselves, but *we will never exhaust the program*. Every slogan, every one of the Steps, and every part of any Step can always be learned on a deeper level. Spirit seeks depth. Our spirits are always urging us to go deeper, get more honest, reach higher, and embrace the Promises more fully.

Back in Week 13, you studied the diagram of the goalposts illustrating the movement from active addiction into sobriety and recovery. Now you can use that same diagram to envision the movement from knowing to being, from knowledge to wisdom, from thinking about to *being* about. Making that leap from the left goalpost to the right is all about being *teachable*.

ANY SUGGESTIONS?

The importance of becoming teachable was emphasized long ago by the program director of a treatment center. His name was Chuck H.

Chuck was a savvy guy. He'd been around for many years and knew all about what's called the "alcoholic personality."

One of his best tricks was gathering together all the folks who were in their first week of treatment and asking them this question: "Do any of you have any suggestions about how to make this program better?"

The response was always the same. Nearly *everyone* came up with suggestions.

Then Chuck made his point: "You don't know a thing about treatment and recovery. You just got here. Your job is *not* to make suggestions about how to run things. Your job is to be quiet, listen, and learn. Your best thinking got you here," he'd say. "God gave you two ears and only one mouth for a reason. You need to listen twice as much as you need to talk. So concentrate on being teachable. You have a lot to learn."

There is indeed a lot to learn in the fifty-two weeks of this book. The information might be simple, but taking it in is not always easy. In fact, it is very rarely easy. Many things that must be learned are "hard truths"—truths we'd just as soon not think about too much. Why? Once we are carried from the left side of the goalpost to the right side by the gift of "hitting bottom" (Week 13), *we are still the same person.* We have the same habits of delusion and denial, the same habits of stinking thinking, the same habitual insanity (Week 10), and the same habit of isolation (weeks 8 and 9).

Learning a different way out and around these thorny roadblocks requires that we become teachable. It requires that we get serious about becoming honest, open, and willing. Put those three together, and you are looking at being teachable.

BECOMING TEACHABLE

Listed below are three markers of teachability. Use them to consider just how teachable you are.

Listen

It's more than just possible to "be at a meeting" but not really be there at all. Someone once said that until he opened his heart and mind and became teachable, he might as well have sent his dog to sit in on the meeting. He was getting about as much out of the meetings, speakers, and sponsors as his dog would.

Do you ever think of taking a pen and paper into your meetings? Many do. They say that if they don't write down the jewels of wisdom born of experience floating around the meetings, they can never remember them.

What if every day you disciplined yourself (Week 4) to write down a couple of things you learned about recovery, either from reflection on your own life or from what someone else did or said? Just think of the Book of Wisdom you'd quickly compile!

Wisdom, like faith, comes from listening.

Learn

What's the lesson? Whether any event is positive or negative, the key question is *what did I learn from it?* Any lesson we don't or won't learn is an opportunity lost. The consequence is another trip "back to the classroom."

Ask yourself: If an event was good, what made it good? If an event was terrible and full of pain, what made it that way? If a mistake was made, what's the lesson? *Being teachable isn't about teaching, it's about learning.* Over and over and over again—so what's the lesson?

• • •

Randy is twenty-eight years sober. At one time, he even went to counselor's training. These days, he goes to dozens of meetings and is a spouting volcano of quotes and Big Book references. There's no question that Randy is a good man. But when it comes to relationships, he could use a good dose of "teachability."

Not long ago, Randy told his group that his most recent relationship "went to hell in a handbasket." (Not surprisingly, he hadn't said anything to his group before or while he was getting enmeshed in the relationship. He failed the work of Week 11.)

The problem was that the woman he got involved with—though "in program"—was still drinking and "occasionally" relapsing back into her cocaine addiction. "But she sounded so good in meetings," Randy said. She also refused to give up her connection with her using friends whom she "just couldn't quit."

When someone in the group asked Randy, "Well, what's the lesson?" He said, "I'm still working on that. I don't know why God put us together." Another group member remarked that he didn't think God was in the dating business. Randy, however, wasn't having that. He was still ten miles beyond positive that this relationship was all about "God's will."

Lean On

Some lessons are harder to learn than others. For many of us, the most difficult are those concerning intimacy. Why is that? Probably because we've lived so long in isolation that we've built strong walls of thinking and acting in utter self-contempt to protect ourselves. That's why we find being wanted, accepted, and loved a huge hill to climb. We can and do love; that's no problem. The problem is in accepting that *we* are loved.

Some of us would gladly exhaust ourselves to be of service to others. Yet when *we're* the ones who need to receive help and hope, we run like scalded dogs. (Like Randy, we tend to let our groups into our life only after it's too late.)

Recovery means leading a spiritual life. A truly spiritual life is as much about receiving as it is giving, as much about leaning on as it is about being the one who's leaned on, as much about telling our secrets as it is about being the willing shoulder and ear that others tell their secrets to. How well do we allow ourselves to be ministered to? Are we willing to lean on anyone?

MAKE IT REAL

Make a pact with yourself. For at least a week, commit to the daily discipline of logging what you've learned through the practice of each of the following:

- LISTENING: To whom?
- LEARNING: What lesson did you learn either from another, from nature, or by paying attention to your own life?
- LEAN ON: (This is hard!) Whom have you let into your life? Whom have you connected to? What happened?

ACTION STEPS

Why do some people never seem to learn? Some are know-it-alls. Others are so afraid of failure that they make only a halfhearted effort. And some "don't get it" simply because they "don't want it"—or at least not enough. Opening ourselves to learning—perhaps for the first time in our lives—is crucial to ongoing recovery.

WRITE: (two or three paragraphs if you can, on the following topics. Give personal examples.)
1. A lesson you learned as a result of a negative experience.
2. A lesson you learned as a result of a positive experience.

SHARE: (with your group or sponsor)
1. One or two ideas for becoming a better student.
2. Explain how a tendency to isolate has handicapped your ability/willingness to learn.

CONSCIOUS CONTACT: Every day ask your Higher Power to remove your barriers to learning.

REACH OUT: Thank someone in your group whose sharing you have listened to and benefited from.

• • •

• **WEEK 20** •

Courage

Why is courage the final attitude on our list?

The answer is this: Courage is not a virtue among other virtues. It is the foundation from which all virtue comes.

Courage doesn't mean going forward in the absence of fear, but rather going forward in the face of fear. And there are many times on the recovery journey, in the first year or any other year, that require going forward in the presence of fear.

Remember my suggestion that you envision these fifty-two weeks in the shape of a wheel or hoop rather than as a linear list? Think of a wheel with spokes. Every segment is connected to every other segment. The life within the wheel flows both forward and backward, sometimes jumping to a number far down the line, then back to Week 2, or 3, or 16. The same is true when we think about courage, fear, and tough situations that must be faced. In the flow of a hoop or wheel, you can envision that hope lies just beyond fear. Yet we must have power to move from fear to hope. If we cannot access that power, we cannot reach hope. We also need to trust that hope will be there for us, and this takes courage—sometimes blind courage. At times, all you can do is row out onto the river of your life and say to yourself, "I don't know how this is going to turn out, or even if I can do it at all—but I'm willing to give it my best shot. I'm willing to step up and do the 'next right thing' no matter how unfamiliar and frightening it feels. I'm resolved to standing firm and trusting that hope lies ahead of me."

The linkage suggested by the wheel goes forward to the section in this book on spirituality, and backward to weeks 13, 14, and 15. It's all spiritual. *Recovery is all spiritual.* That is why we're told that what we have to share with others is our "experience, strength, and hope."

Recovery is not an armchair theory. It is life. And life is grounded in experience. Fortunately for us, the experience of millions upon millions of people in recovery demonstrates that there is strength to be had in the program. Our hope comes from that strength. To hope for any outcome without having the strength or resources to make that outcome possible is simple foolishness. The experience of the millions of people in recovery is that working a program is anything but foolish.

But doing the work takes courage—which is invoking the strength that provides the hope. And it is hope that provides the endurance—which in turn provides lifelong recovery, one day at a time.

We need courage to face our particular brand of insanity (Week 10). It takes courage to stay connected when we're drowning in guilt and shame. It takes courage to practice honesty, gratitude, endurance, and teachability (weeks 15 through 19) until these new attitudes take root. It takes courage to "turn our lives over to the care of God." For us, to trust anything having to do with caring, especially about someone caring for us, takes "a Power not of this earth."

There is only one thing harder than recovery, and that is *not* recovering. (Once again, look back to Week 4 for "what's lost" and Week 15 for "what's gained.")

The fact is that recovery is hard. Many people, especially those new to recovery, run into one of recovery's "hard things" and often exclaim in surprise, "This is hard!"

Yet how in the world could recovery be easy? Creating new habits of attitudes, staying connected, meeting a loving Higher Power, and doing what it takes to move ahead into the life of the Promises—even if it is rewarding beyond all imagining—is hard. Any important new effort is hard. Especially if the "old" is hedged with rabid attack dogs of laziness and despair. Nothing short of real courage is required to endure, to press onward until the danger, at least for now, is passed.

But all of us who pursue "progress, not perfection" will find—if we stay connected to our "team," both human and divine—that they will show up and take us through the fire again. And again and again. We will find that it is in acknowledging our weakness, in surrender and acceptance, that we find our true strength. And that strength allows hope to shine above any power that could blot it out.

MAKE IT REAL

Courage in living the program—where have you seen it? In what ways have you lived it? What form and shape did it take? What did it tell you?

List examples of courage you have seen. Then describe the lesson—what *you* learned—by witnessing these acts of courage. *Do not skip this exercise.*

ACTION STEPS

How can we overcome our fear of the difficult? For many of us, hopelessness is a long-standing habit. If we're willing, however, our Higher Power, working through our Twelve Step program, will relieve us of that terrible burden. How? Through acceptance and surrender, one day at a time, one step at a time.

WRITE: (two or three paragraphs if you can, on the following topics. Give personal examples.)
1. Tell about a time when you were able to "go forward in the face of fear."
2. Explain why "courage is the foundation from which all virtue comes."

SHARE: (with your group or sponsor)
1. As best you can, identify and describe two or three of your greatest fears.
2. Your personal commitment to undertake a small act of courage that you've been avoiding.

CONSCIOUS CONTACT: Thank your Higher Power for "having your back" in your quest for personal courage.

REACH OUT: After a meeting, congratulate a member of your group who's shown courage in facing a difficulty.

• • •

The Steps

• WEEK 21 •

Why the Steps Work

A number of good study guides on the Steps are available. Many clubs and groups also conduct classes on the Steps for new members. The Fellowship is blessed with a good many individuals who have made it their life's mission to teach others how to work the Steps. I strongly encourage you to plug into *any* source of support in working the Steps.

This book, however, is going to look at the Steps in a different way. Rather than focus on *how* to work the Steps, we'll discuss *why* the Steps work as they do (if we truly work them). This focus is in keeping with the book's overall goal of helping you "lift the lid" on recovery to see *why* the individual parts work.

Experience proves that the better that newcomers (and retreads, too!) understand *why* we do what we do in recovery, the more they are empowered to do—and to keep doing what it takes to stay on that right side of the goalpost.

AA asserts that people don't have to know *why* they drink to stop drinking. That's absolutely true. But it is also my belief—again, backed up by experience—that many who relapse never fully understood the *process* of moving from active addiction to sobriety and then on to the life of the Promises. They never fully understood *why* they needed to do what they were asked to do. They failed to endure (Week 18). They stopped doing the small things that make the Big Thing—ongoing recovery—possible.

Go back and review the seven questions in Week 14. Review, share, and teach them to others until the connections between all the various parts of moving from active addiction to recovery and then into the

Promises make perfect sense. Challenge yourself to truly understand "the exact nature" of your disease *and* the specific steps necessary to escape isolation and the prison of self-contempt that addiction causes.

> **READER ALERT:** *What comes next requires a bit of thought. Take your time with this material. See how the following ideas fit with* **your own experience of recovery and sharing with others.** *Please do the work. The payoff is a thousand times worth the effort.*

RECOVERY EQUALS REGAINED HUMANITY

In your journey of recovery, where are you starting from? Generally, in any endeavor (none more important than recovery), the point where your thinking and perceptions *start* affects where you will finish. The more you understand going into a venture, the greater your success.

When it comes to recovery, a good starting point is understanding who we are exactly: *We are human beings before we are addicts.* We're human beings who happen to be addicts, not addicts who happen to be human beings.

Why is that such an important concept? Because active addiction is about more than taking a drink or drug. It is behavior that diminishes, damages, and ultimately destroys our humanity. Recovery, then, is not simply the removal of the addictive substance—which alone can never restore and repair the damage that active addiction has created. Rather, true recovery is the process of regaining our humanity—that is, our spirituality.

That's why it's enormously helpful at the very start of the recovery process to understand that our journey *must* go beyond achieving sobriety. Sobriety, of course, must come first. But the journey must *continue* from that starting place. Why? Because "clean and sober" alone cannot make you healthy and happy. Sobriety only allows you to see the destruction that addiction has caused in your life and the lives of your loved ones. It leaves you face to face with your pain without the "medication" of drugs or alcohol. True, enduring recovery includes doing the work it takes to heal that pain and to meet our core human needs.

The two deepest needs of every human being are (1) to love and be loved and (2) to be accepted and feel a sense of belonging. These needs are called lots of different names, but ultimately they all mean the same thing.

Anything that prevents us from meeting these needs creates isolation—an accurate description of alcoholism and addiction, as we have seen. (Review your work in weeks 4 and 5.)

• • •

The values underlying active addiction (Week 9) block spirituality and prevent us from meeting those needs that are basic to a life worthy of a human being.

The purpose of working the Steps is to breach those walls that isolate us. Doing so is the only way we can cultivate the values that make us most human—values such as the ten identified in Week 10. That's why the Steps work—because they have the power, if consistently worked, to release us from the prison of self that's been built by addiction.

The values behind addiction create isolation.

The values behind recovery create connection.

In a very fundamental sense, recovery—and the working of the Steps that is at the heart of recovery—is a matter of being released to "go home."

What does this process look like in real life? Here are a few snapshots and sound bites describing what "going home" may look like. Read what these people in recovery have to say about where their recovery took them:

- "I'm just grateful to wake up alive every morning. I should have been dead a thousand times. After all that, I never thought I deserved to be alive."
- "I'm able to have friends now! My heart had turned to a piece of stone during my drinking. I never thought anyone would ever want me around again."
- "God is now my friend. Before, I blamed God for everything that was wrong with my life. But it wasn't God. It was me. Now

that I am taking responsibility for the outcomes in my life, I've
been able to discover a new relationship with God."

- "For the first time in my life, I am making free decisions. I
never made free decisions before. I just did what my addiction
told me to do."
- "I now feel I have access to all the good things that make life
worth the effort. I never did before, and it turned me into a
raging idiot."
- "Beyond all doubt, guilt, fear, and shame, I am starting to accept
that I am worth something. People actually want me around
now!"
- "I was in active addiction for forty-six years. My gods were my
pistol and my addiction. I never did anything for anyone else.
Now I would do anything I could to help another suffering
addict."
- "These days, I have something to offer others. Not long ago, someone asked *me* to be their sponsor. Who would have guessed?"

Clearly, for these people, recovery is the journey back to their hearts,
back to their humanity, back home. Is this not your experience?

MAKE IT REAL

The goal of this week's work is so vital that we will keep building on it through Week 25. The purpose is to highlight and make
powerfully clear the connection between working the Steps and
"going home."

So, whether you are most comfortable calling this connection to
your core "homecoming," "serenity," "peace," "spirituality," "fellowship," or some other term—just *do the work* of reflecting, going inside,
and looking at your story and the stories of others. Then express
yourself in writing by answering these three questions in detail:

1. What are five specific examples from your own story about
how recovery has taken you back to your humanity—which is
to say back to your heart, back to loving and allowing yourself

to be loved, back to experiencing acceptance by others and belonging with others?

2. What are five specific things you've learned by looking around and listening to others describe how their recovery work (working the Steps) has taken them back to their humanity?

3. How would you explain to someone else how recovery and working the Steps is all about "going home"?

Please do this work! *Do not skimp on the energy and effort you put into answering these three questions. Take your time until it becomes crystal clear that, because you are first of all a human being, recovery is the process of restoring your humanity.*

The payoff for working the Steps is enormous: The poisonous walls of isolation around our hearts break down and we *regain our humanity.*

Personally, I have kept track of the blessings of recovery for more than forty years. Every day I write down an example of the blessings, the going home, the regained humanity that recovery brings into my life and the lives of those around me. It is always astonishing! Every day I witness amazing grace.[2]

Do this work and you, too, will be amazed.

ACTION STEPS

Why doesn't "clean and sober" automatically make you "healthy and happy"? Because of how addiction has damaged your basic humanity. Traveling the long path from the train wreck of addiction to the life of the Promises requires that you regain what you have lost.

WRITE: (two or three paragraphs if you can, on the following topics. Give personal examples.)

1. Explain what it's worth to you to make free decisions (instead of doing what your addiction tells you to do).

---

[2] A fully developed treatment of these ideas and their implications can be found in the Hazelden book *Destination Joy: Moving Beyond Fear, Loss, and Trauma in Recovery* by Earnie Larsen. Or, log on to www.changeisachoice.com.

2. Describe two things you might do to help other suffering addicts.

SHARE: (with your group or sponsor)
1. Explain your understanding of the statement "Working the Steps means going home."
2. Talk about two specific actions you are now taking to escape or avoid isolation.

CONSCIOUS CONTACT: On a daily basis, ask your Higher Power to speak to you through your group.

REACH OUT: Look around your meetings for someone who seems to be a loner. Offer some form of fellowship—a greeting, a word of encouragement, an invitation to lunch, for example.

• • •

• **WEEK 22** •

What We Practice
When We Work the Steps

Once you've internalized the material in Week 21, it's time to take a deeper look at why the Steps are as they are and why they work.

The key idea this week is that *each of the Steps promotes at least one essential value.* Working the Steps creates a *habit* of that value, which is what breaks down the walls of isolation created by the addiction. This explains why the Steps work—because *we change* while we are working them. We *become* better as we *do* better, and we enable ourselves to do even better. It is right there, in that gradual spiritual transformation, that we become increasingly able to claim the twenty-four-hour reprieve that Twelve Step recovery offers.

Does that make sense? We become what we practice. When we practiced the values underlying addiction, we became fixated on the left side of the goalposts (weeks 8 through 10).

But when we practice the values that underlie recovery by working the Steps (Week 14), those positive values transform into attitudes (weeks 16 through 20) that become the foundation of a "new normal." The more we "earn our recovery" (Week 14), the more automatically we'll believe, think, feel, and carry out the actions that are the faces of active recovery. It is through this kind of focused, consistent work that character defects fade away and character assets emerge.

This doesn't mean we can then get complacent and take our recovery for granted. Mess with the beast of addiction, and it will barge through the slightest crack in the door and take us down (Week 5). This explains why some people relapse after many years in the Fellowship. Life gets too easy. They forget the "exact nature" of our disease (Week 4).

Addiction's best trick is to convince us that it doesn't exist—at least not in *my* life. Addiction's second best trick is to convince us that it is on vacation and no longer interested in us. This is when addiction starts puffing little shots of poison smoke (called stinking thinking) up our noses and into our brains. The bottom line: *complacency kills.*

Do you remember the recovery values introduced in Week 14? It's no coincidence that these same values are linked to the values that the Steps foster.

This list of values is not "official" or absolute. The Steps are bottomless, and different values could be drawn from each of the Twelve Steps. But the ones listed below work well enough. The point is that practicing the Steps is practicing the values that pierce the shell around our humanity that prevents us from meeting our deepest needs. Once again, practicing these new values is how we break down the walls of isolation that make us easy prey to the lion of addiction.

Here, then, is the list illustrating how the values are linked to the various Steps. If other values seem to fit the various Steps better for you—or if it seems to you that each Step fosters more than one value—great; use whatever works for you. Make your own list. The important thing to understand is that "working the Steps" is not some kind of magic activity that "somehow" leads to quality recovery. The Steps are *tools.* When a competent worker uses the right tool for the right job, the job gets done. The Steps are a *map.* Follow it and you will not get lost. The Steps are *signposts.* Go where they direct you, and you'll never end up back on the left-hand side of the goalpost.

- Step One fosters ACCEPTANCE. It enables us to get honest and to take seriously what is *really* happening in our lives. Acceptance is the antidote to denial. A person cannot practice Step One and remain isolated and imprisoned inside his or her own world of active addiction.
- Step Two fosters FAITH. It allows us to get out of self by an act of faith. This usually doesn't happen all at once—that's what "came to believe" means. But in Step Two, we begin to open up to the idea that there is an almighty power available beyond

our own puny efforts. *If* "that Power were sought," we could and would be relieved of our addiction—*if he were sought.* A person cannot practice Step Two and remain isolated and imprisoned inside his or her own world of active addiction.

- Step Three fosters TRUST. It empowers us not only to open up to the possibility of a Power other than and greater than ourselves, but to make a decision to turn our lives over to the "care of God as we understand Him." *Trust is required to escape isolation.* A person cannot practice Step Three and remain isolated and imprisoned inside his or her own world of active addiction.

- Step Four fosters HONESTY. It enables us to look at ourselves, see the truth, and tell the truth. Character defects block the spirituality that lifts a person out of isolation. Honesty is a key requirement in developing that spirituality. A person cannot practice Step Four and remain imprisoned inside his or her own world of active addiction.

- Step Five fosters COURAGE. It encourages us to take the heroic step of building connections with "God, self, and another human being" within which and through which the power to escape active addiction (and keep on going) is found. A person cannot practice Step Five and remain imprisoned inside his or her own world of active addiction.

- Step Six fosters WILLINGNESS. It readies us to be open to a new way of living without allowing our old character defects to help us hide from what we find troubling and dangerous. A person cannot practice Step Six and remain imprisoned inside his or her own world of active addiction.

- Step Seven fosters HUMILITY. It enables us to ask for help. It helps us to accept the reality that we are *not* God. It empowers us to own and act on the idea that there is a better way to live than hiding in our character defects. A person cannot practice Step Seven and remain imprisoned inside his or her own world of active addiction.

- Step Eight fosters FORGIVENESS. It allows us to accept the truth that we hurt others while we were living in the insanity of our active addiction. For those wrongs we are responsible, and our personal spirituality demands that we become willing to take appropriate action. A person cannot practice Step Eight and remain imprisoned inside his or her own world of active addiction.

- Step Nine fosters FREEDOM. It helps us rise up to a higher level of behavior than blaming others and running from our responsibilities. Making amends to those we have harmed creates a greater level of freedom than we have ever known (or imagined) while trapped in active addiction. A person cannot practice Step Nine and remain imprisoned inside his or her own world of active addiction.

- Step Ten fosters PERSEVERANCE. On a daily basis, it strengthens the attitude of endurance by focusing our attention on how we are living—specifically in regard to where we are most in danger of allowing the insanity of active addiction back into our lives. A person cannot practice Step Ten and remain imprisoned in his or her world of active addiction.

- Step Eleven fosters PATIENCE. It helps us to put the unrolling of our lives in the hands of the God of our understanding. That means accepting that we are not in charge of everything in our lives, and that we often *do not know* what is best for us or others. This Step fosters the attitude of letting God be God and being patient as God works his will in this world. A person cannot practice Step Eleven and remain imprisoned in his or her own world of active addiction.

- Step Twelve fosters LOVE. It develops and deepens the belief and the attitude that if these Steps were practiced (the map followed and the tools used), then love itself would be the standard by which our lives would be guided and measured. It reveals the truth that the right side of the goalpost is ultimately about nothing but love. *Recovery is love gained. Relapse is love lost.* A person cannot practice Step Twelve and remain under the crushing heel of active addiction.

As mentioned earlier in this week's work, any number of values could be linked to the Steps. The point is simply that *positive recovery values are inherent in the Steps.* Practice of the Steps *is* practice of the values. The question is never about the importance of uninterrupted sobriety; that goes without saying. The real question is "How is that ongoing sobriety best achieved?" *Recovery must and does go far beyond sobriety alone.*

Connect the dots. Reflect on the work suggested in this week's material on why the Steps work. Look into your own life in recovery. Observe the lives of those around you. By all means, sign up for any classes on understanding and working the Steps. *By all means!* But also see if the practice of positive values is not the river, so to speak, running under and through your working of the Steps specifically and all of recovery in general.

MAKE IT REAL

Attach a value to each of the Steps. Clarify for yourself how practicing that value is always necessary to break free from the isolation of spiritual bankruptcy.

Write out for yourself how *this* practice of *this* value in *this* Step is actually taking you out of spiritual bankruptcy and into the solution of spiritual connection. The more specific and personal you can make it, the better. Look at the connections you are making. Ask yourself, "What's the lesson here? What am I looking at? What skill or strength or ability am I gaining that is essential for my recovery?"

Share your insights with others and listen as they share their insights with you. What are you hearing? What lesson are they revealing?

ACTION STEPS

Even little kids know that tools are necessary if you need to pound a nail or cut wood. Thinking of the Steps as the tools they are can help you get busy doing the work that needs to be done.

WRITE: (two or three paragraphs if you can, on the following topics. Give personal examples.)

1. Explain why trust and humility are two important recovery values. Give examples.
2. Explain the meaning of "We become what we practice."

SHARE: (with your group or sponsor)
1. Talk about a difficult situation you may be facing that concerns honesty, patience, or any other recovery value.
2. Tell about a new habit you're developing that is promoting your recovery.

CONSCIOUS CONTACT: Thank your Higher Power for "having your back" in all the twenty-four-hour periods you've been sober. Ask for continued support.

PRACTICE: On a regular basis, take ten minutes out of your day to *listen* to what your Higher Power is saying to you.

● ● ●

• WEEK 23 •

The Power of Love and Love Denied

Every so often, as I present this material in person, someone throws out a challenging question. It comes in various forms, such as, "What you're talking about sounds too easy. All this talk about the heart, going home, attitudes, fixing the inside, spirituality, love—it's all nice enough. But *my* addiction is made of the stuff of nightmares. Its heart is blacker than night. I'm in a dogfight for my life here. I need redder meat than what you seem to be talking about. I need a tougher version of recovery."

There is nothing easy about the work I'm talking about. It only sounds easy to those who have not yet walked the road I'm describing. Especially in the first year, we have a lot of hard work to do— because the simple truth is that *recovery cannot take hold in a life that's a mess.* Recovery can't take root or grow in a life mired in fear, rage, anxiety, frustration, guilt, grief, loneliness, and shame.

Recovery is spiritual, and spirituality is about connections— relationships with our Higher Power, self, and others. A person who has never figured out how to make relationships work—or why they consistently fail—faces serious obstacles in recovery.

Why? Because character defects block our ability to initiate or build healthy relationships, which in turn blocks spirituality, which in turn blocks recovery. Shining a light into the dark corners of our character defects requires nothing less than heavy-duty courage.

If we lack the courage to go within and honestly meet what is both healthy and broken about our lives, we'll never be able to surrender to the "care of God *as we understood Him.*" We will never be able to challenge all that has come to be "normal" in an active addiction, and the "better way" that recovery offers can never be long embraced. Temporarily, it can be. Some people do gain sobriety *for a time.* But the physical disposition to addiction, once again triggered by the fang and claw of "unfinished business," will lead to relapse again and again.

The Steps tell us this. The Steps have their own voice. They are the map that directs us where to go and shows us what must be done.

Steps One through Three set the solid foundation on which Twelve Step recovery is based. I fervently believe that without an ever-growing conscious connection to one's Higher Power, sobriety and recovery are unattainable. Either we tap into that power not of this earth, or the power of our alcoholism or addiction—which is very much of this earth—will consume us. Reflect on the shorthand of the first three Steps: *I can't, he can, so I let him.*

Step Four doesn't tell us to go to school and get a Ph.D. in psychology. It doesn't say we should build a string of businesses and get rich. Nor does it say we need to get smarter or become more socially acceptable or learn better manners. The voice of the Steps tells us to go *within.* It says to identify our character defects so they can be removed—or at least diminished to the extent that they lose the power to prevent us from "going home."

Remember, our character defects block the growth of spirituality that alone enables us to stay connected in an honest, deep manner with our Higher Power, self, and others (review Week 11).

All the Steps are action steps. They all help us establish a spirituality that is strong enough to counter the terrible mental, physical, emotional, and spiritual destruction caused by an active addiction.

Let me be clear: Whoever refuses to take seriously and deal directly with the character defects that strangle spirituality courts disaster (review Week 4). We hunger for spirituality. When that hunger is not fed, we are left with a hungry heart that cannot withstand the rush of addiction. The combination of the physical disposition plus a trigger event that was not identified, understood, or countered will mow you down every time. Character defects are the matches set to the fuse of the trigger event.

A hungry heart is a heart that has yet to find a home. It doesn't know where it belongs because it lacks connections—it lacks love. Because recovery is about more than achieving sobriety—it is about whole-life healing and transformation—the bottom line is that love and love denied are our only two options. *A life able to embrace love flourishes. A life unable to embrace love withers.* Active addiction is about as good an example of a withered life as you'll ever see.

Does your story not tell you this? When you look in the mirror of your story, is this not the image peering back at you?

●   ●   ●

Ann can't stay sober. She makes a good start, gets maybe a year or so, but then she relapses. While sober, Ann goes to meetings and, as she says, "lives for service work." She has friends in the program, and many say she's the best friend anyone could ever have—as long as the friendship is based on Ann giving to and helping others. When it comes to *accepting* care from others, she doesn't do so well.

There are large parts of Ann's life she's not willing to look at, let alone accept. She laughs when she shares tragic events from her childhood. She *always* smiles. Ann is married, but she makes a comic routine out of constantly saying her husband is on her hit list—along with all the other people she can't stand.

Occasionally, someone in her group brings up something Ann might want to take a look at, or openly confronts her about all the negativity behind her smiles. Whenever that happens, Ann waves it off, dances around, and refuses to listen. She can give a great talk on being "honest, open, and willing," but her manner says that those guests have never sat at her table.

It really doesn't take long to see that, behind all the smiles, she is drowning in tears and loneliness.

Ann relapsed again last week. This time she ended up in the hospital. She'll be back to group soon. When someone asks her, "What did you learn this time around?" Ann will smile, lean in close, and say something like, "I don't know. What do *you* think I needed to learn?" She makes a game out of saving her life.

For Ann, all the "love talk" and "going home talk" is diversion. She can talk the talk all day. But when it comes to gut-level honesty, the courage to honestly trust, and the attitude of being teachable, she hasn't even begun to walk the walk (weeks 16 through 20). Ann hasn't even started to work on developing honesty and trust, so she is paying the price for this failure.

• • •

After many twelve- to eighteen-month sober periods followed by relapse and another start, Frank got tired of it all. After his last relapse, he found a place he thought was sufficiently secluded and took a razor blade to his wrist. He said his only thought as the blood spurted out was "Thank God, I'm out of it."

But that place wasn't secluded enough. Frank was spotted leaning against a fence, soaked in his own blood. Emergency services were called, and he was saved. Or was he?

Frank's in a new long-term treatment program now. Of course, he's been in *many* long-term treatment programs. He's a wizard at treatment. Frank could run his own treatment program if he wanted. There isn't really much new for Frank to learn. Could it be his problem isn't what he does not know, but rather what he is not willing to face?

Like many people in the program, Frank is witty and charming, and he has a lot of friends. At least, he has many people who are friendly *to him*. But how many people does Frank allow to be *his* friend? Like Ann, he'll do anything to help someone—other than himself.

There is emptiness at Frank's core. It's the old "hole in the soul" so often spoken of in the program. But talking about it isn't enough. Something must be *done* about it. Connections—real connections— *must* be made. Old habits and attitudes *must* be confronted. They *must* be challenged. New ways to deal with emptiness and old frustrations *must* be learned. Surrender *must* be made.

Some people in the program seem to do less than Frank and still get by. But *do* they, really? Who knows? The program tells us that "half measures avail us nothing." And halfway surely isn't going to make it for Frank. He has a half-paralyzed hand to prove it, and an equally paralyzing fear of what the program asks of him—which is to *deal with your insides.*

Frank, like Ann, kind of likes all the "love talk." He's given powerful talks on the power of fellowship and how real and strong it must be. But talking is just talking. Only doing is doing.

MAKE IT REAL

How about you? Are there secrets still hidden from your program? Are there corners you won't go into or allow anyone else to know about? What of the "hole in your soul"? Is there one? Have you often relapsed because of it? Do you know the character defects that threaten to pull you down? Do you have a hungry heart? How are the connections in your life? Are they in place? Are they strong? Are you feeding them on a daily basis?

Choose any one or more of the questions above. Answer them honestly. Share what you find with another. What did you learn?

ACTION STEPS

Exposure is scary—especially exposure to one's own self! All of us have a dark corner or two we'd rather not explore. But, through the genius of "one day at a time," it's possible—and immensely rewarding—to face the truth about ourselves. Our very survival depends on it.

WRITE: (two or three paragraphs if you can, on the following topics. Give personal examples.)
1. What aspects of your character (what defects) are most difficult to admit?
2. Give three reasons why connections are so important.

SHARE: (with your group or sponsor)
1. Tell about a "half measure" you've tried to substitute for an honest effort.
2. Talk about any difficulties you may have in connecting to others.

CONSCIOUS CONTACT: Tell your Higher Power a secret about yourself that you've never been willing to share with anyone else. (He doesn't need to hear it; *you* need to say it.)

• • •

• WEEK 24 •

The Steps and a Spiritual Awakening

Let's look at the Twelfth Step. Say the first words aloud: "Having had a spiritual awakening as the result of these Steps . . ." A person could meditate on the meaning and importance of these words forever and never plumb the depths.

Of all the good counsel that could have been built into the Steps, why focus on a "spiritual awakening"? And what exactly *is* the connection between working the Steps and having that spiritual awakening?

From the months of work you've put into this program so far, does the answer pop up bright and clear? Do you and your group see the connection clearly?

What's the problem? What's the solution? How does one get to and then stay in the solution?

In Step Twelve, the answer is right in front of us. If we practice the Steps, we will experience spiritual awakenings—and those awakenings surface (some would say explode) at the points where the shell around our hearts is pierced.

Have you noticed that among many recovering alcoholics/addicts a kind of "can you top this?" game often develops? One after another, stories from each person's drunkalog come rolling out, maybe for the hundredth time. There's always a lot of head shaking and laughter around the stories. Some of them are funny in kind of a black humor way. Yet while these folks are not the least embarrassed or hesitant about putting the misery and agony of their active addiction on display, many of these same people would shudder at the suggestion to share the spiritual side of their story. Telling others about their stories of "the bounce," of hitting bottom and climbing out the other side, seems out of bounds or suspect. It's as if they feel they fit in—like one of the guys or gals—by telling their drunkalog, but they fear looking like an oddball or "one of *those*" if they talk about the spiritual awakenings they've experienced.

Does that seem odd to you?

The language of the Twelfth Step is very clear: Spiritual awakenings *are* the result of working the Steps. And when the dots are connected between the problem, the solution, and the sweet spot of staying connected, it becomes obvious that the various spiritual awakenings we experience as we move deeper into the program are the very lifeblood of recovery.

So let's reflect on our story and find those spiritual awakenings. Let's celebrate them to high heaven! Go back to Week 4 and review the incredible injury and loss addiction has cost you. Then line up these losses next to the spiritual awakenings you have experienced (either slowly or explosively). Talk about a reason to celebrate! There it is, right in front of us.

On one side is the terrible cost. On the other side is the lifesaving reward. In recovery, we are living the reward.

Not long ago, one of our group mates brought two large X-ray pictures to a meeting. Three years ago, he'd been diagnosed with a cancerous tumor in his throat. One of those X-rays clearly showed the tumor. But his tumor had gone into remission. In fact, it had absolutely disappeared! The second X-ray showed the same area—but this picture was clear. There was no dark outline of the tumor that so clearly had been there earlier.

The man could hardly keep from jumping up and down on his chair. He was filled with gratitude—overwhelmed that such a marvelous, miraculous thing had happened to him. "Just look at these two X-rays!" he kept shouting. "You want to see a miracle, here it is!"

Of course, everyone was happy for him. But there was more than one miracle going on in that room.

What if everyone at that meeting were shown two X-rays—one depicting all the misery, suffering, and failure caused by their addiction, and another outlining all the blessings and spiritual awakenings that person was now experiencing in recovery. Examining those two X-rays side by side would be proof of a first-class miracle. Everyone in recovery has a reason to stand on his or her chair and celebrate their miracle.

SPIRITUAL AWAKENINGS

The work you did in weeks 21 through 23 allowed you to see more clearly *why* working the Steps creates spiritual awakenings. Now let's look at *what* those awakenings have been for you.

Perhaps a good way to do this work is to think about your "recovery timeline." How did it start and what changes have you seen along the way? What awakenings have you experienced that became a path lit up by a thousand luminaries leading you away from isolation and into the life-saving embrace of the Fellowship?

Let's talk about hitting bottom: No recovery starts without it. Hitting bottom is a gift. In fact, brokenness itself is a gift without which there is no hope. What was hitting bottom like for *you*? How did it happen? When did it happen? How did you "awaken" to the truth that enough is enough? What finally made you sick and tired of being sick and tired?

Who was the first person who reached out a hand to you in recovery? Was it through an intervention? Or was it maybe someone who answered your call to Intergroup? Or was it that "angel at the door" so many of us met when we, terrified and beaten, were driven to our first meeting? Or was it a counselor in treatment? Who first welcomed you to the program?

When was your first awakening to the astounding fact that "I am wanted"? That "I belong here"? When and where did you first realize, "This is my group. They know if I fail to make a meeting. If they don't see me around, someone will call me and say, 'Hey, we miss you. Do you need a ride? Get your butt back to group'"?

When was the first time you experienced that there really, truly was *hope*? When did you first awaken to the fact that "I can do this"? When did you first leap (or allow yourself to be carried) over the chasm of doubt and defeat into the belief that "If I work my program, my program will protect me"?

At what point did it dawn on you that *you* had something to give? When did you first realize that the power of the program was in you, and that *you* were called to share it with another? What was that like? How did it feel? What was the lesson?

When did you first and finally "come to believe" that there was a Higher Power who cared for you? How many times did you hear and read the Third Step, "Made a decision to turn our lives over to the care of God as we understood Him"? *Care.* Not power or intelligence or justice—but to the *care* of God. When did you first glimpse that God was your copilot and always had been beside you, offering his care?

There are dozens of spiritual awakenings that support us. As long as we "work the Steps," we will continually have spiritual awakenings. Each one is a strand that twines around earlier awakenings, together becoming an unbreakable cable of connection to our Higher Power, self, and others. Each one leads us further into our recovery.

MAKE IT REAL

Again—please do this work. Take your time. Reflect on each aspect of a spiritual awakening. Flesh each one out. Who was there for you? What happened? What did you learn? How was your consciousness changed?

Share your work with others in your group. Listen to the stories of their awakenings. If appropriate, stand on your chair—all of you stand on your chairs—and *celebrate!*

ACTION STEPS

Why is a spiritual awakening so important? To "awaken" is to become *conscious*—to become aware of what's going on and capable of thinking about it. It's the restoration of our full humanity that allows us to "practice these principles in all our affairs."

WRITE: (two or three paragraphs if you can, on the following topics. Give personal examples.)

1. Explain the relationship between working the Steps and experiencing spiritual awakenings.
2. Why do you think so many of us are more comfortable sharing a drunkalog rather than a story about our "bouncing back" after hitting bottom?

SHARE: (with your group or sponsor)
1. An example of a "spiritual awakening" you've experienced.
2. Why hitting bottom can be considered a gift.

CONSCIOUS CONTACT: Ask your Higher Power to help you recognize opportunities to share your experience, strength, and hope.

PRACTICE: Carry a notebook so you can write down your daily awakenings to recovery values.

• • •

• WEEK 25 •

Carry the Message

The second part of the Twelfth Step is all about service work. It's about getting out of self and helping others. It's about carrying the message. The sooner we begin to escape the prison of self, the sooner we begin to recover from the disease of addiction.

But what is the message we're supposed to carry? And how far along in recovery does a person have to be to carry it?

To answer these questions, start by remembering who you were and how you were when you first came—or came back—to the program. How were you feeling? What was going on inside of you? Which of your needs was bleeding all over the floor? What had you lost? (Review Week 4.) What message did you most need to encounter to "get in" and "keep on climbing?"

True service work means getting out of self. And that means, among other things, getting out of yourself as you are *now*. Think back to *who you were* to best understand what message it is you have to give. Look through the eyes of your spirit at who you were then, who you are now, and what most helped you at the very beginning.

Nothing less than love is required. Some of you may wonder, "Is all that love stuff strong enough, or is it all just fluff? Fluff that somehow weakens and distracts from *real* recovery?"

• • •

Meet James. At 350 pounds, James is hard to miss. All his life he's been called "Big James." He's big in a lot of ways. Being on his own from age nine and being a "street baby," as he says, James grew up tough.

He'd lived in twelve foster homes before he finally went out on his own at age sixteen. He was already deep into criminal behavior. James will be the first one to tell you, though, that his life didn't seem criminal to him. It was all he knew. In the world he came from, there weren't any other options.

James did his time in juvenile hall and prisons. He rode with the worst of the outlaw motorcycle gangs. When not in prison, James was a hit man and leg-breaker for a major loan shark and drug king. For the longest time, he said, kneecapping people, breaking other bones, or worse never bothered him. It was just what he did. It was just life.

Miracles happen. In the mysterious, spiritual way it happens, James got sick and tired of being sick and tired. He floated into recovery (as much as a big man like James can "float"), and there his heart was changed. He was picked up from the left-hand side of the goalpost and dropped on the right side of recovery (Week 13), where he found a fellowship he had never imagined existed. As he moved along into recovery, he began having spiritual awakenings (Week 24). Slowly, his inner eyes were opened, and he saw a sweet vision of what life *could be*. Never before had he dared such a dream for himself.

James is functionally illiterate, but he has a Ph.D. in street wisdom. His X-ray vision immediately cuts through any scamming, posing, or game playing (at least what *he* sees as game playing).

One day, James was invited by his sponsor to a fancy recovery celebration hosted by a large treatment center. Besides just celebrating recovery, the highlight of the event was the presentation of an award for academic contribution to the field of recovery. That year the honor went to a statistician who had researched and created a software program for tracking the effectiveness of various treatment programs for different forms of addiction. No doubt the fellow had made a worthy and worthwhile contribution.

For some reason, James's interest was piqued. He wanted to meet this man. So after the presentation was over, James ambled over to this individual, introduced himself, and politely asked a few questions.

Two of James's questions were "Have you ever done service work? Have you ever done a Twelve Step call?"

James said the man didn't understand the question. He said he didn't know what "service work" was. So James thanked him for his time and walked away.

On their way home, James's sponsor asked, "So, did you find out what you wanted to know from him?" James said, "Yeah, but he don't know what counts. He don't know where the dogs are fighting."

Of course, there is a side to treating disease other than what James knows or cares about. Academic research has its place. But recovery is not all or even mostly about professionals conducting research or outcome studies. That's not who has been called to "carry the message" of hope and help to the hopeless and helpless. Those who are called to serve in this precious, mysterious, and miraculous work of recovery are *people who can see with their hearts*. It's those people, whether in the first or fiftieth year, who "know where the dogs are fighting." It's those people who know the difference between the dogma of the program and the spirit of the program—and serve the spirit.

There's a story that has floated around the rooms forever about a long-established, rather rigid group of old-timers. The story goes that at one crowded meeting, mostly of other rather uptight old-timers, a shoeless young man with a scruffy beard, torn jeans, and metal rings all around his face showed up. Supposedly, the noise volume of the room dropped as he walked in. Many of those in attendance were looking at the young man out of the corners of their eyes and wondering, "What is *he* doing here?"

Since no chairs were available, the young man moved to the side and effortlessly slid down the wall until he was sitting on the floor. The oldest of the old-timers, a dignified man leaning on a cane, walked over to the young man, looked down at him, and then—with considerable effort—slid down the wall himself until he was sitting next to the young man. He held out his hand to the young man, said his name, and told him, "I'm glad you are here. You are among friends."

The old-timer knew why the newcomer was there—for the same reason everyone else was there: To find sobriety and the means to stay sober within the Fellowship. That first of all. That above all. That all in all. Everything else was just clutter.

What's the message? Who qualifies to carry that message?

Every organization has two parts: the dogma and the spirit, the law and the spirit of the law, the written word and the lived word. So it is with the Twelve Step Fellowship. So it is with recovery. One is in the head and the other is in the heart. Both are necessary. (That's why there are Twelve Traditions supporting the Twelve Steps.) Both are necessary, but both are certainly not the same.

Recovery is about *living* the Steps, and that is a matter of the heart. It's about the spirit and not just the knowing. It's about knowledge that is pushed to wisdom by the *living* of that knowledge. It's about opening a path from head to heart so the heart, the self, our humanity is able to crawl out from under the insanity of addiction and start climbing upward on the wings of lifesaving connection.

And what does all this have to do with new recovery? *Everything.* Where we start is where we finish. We, your sponsors and coaches, urge you to begin your recovery with the clear understanding that this journey is of the spirit and of the heart. The wisdom we seek can only be found by opening our hearts. It's about caring, even though caring is risky—yes, we can be hurt. But without caring, without the spirit of the old-timer in the story who knew what that young man needed, who knew how to "carry the message of the program to him," there is only a shadow of what's real. Without the spirit, there's only dancing around what is real, and "dancing around" doesn't take a person home. Recovery is about going home.

ACTION STEPS

As recovering addicts, we're painfully aware of our own neediness as well as our past failures to honor our obligations to others. Surely there are better people to "carry the message." But the program teaches us otherwise when it advises, "You have to give it away to keep it."

WRITE: (two or three paragraphs if you can, on the following topics. Give personal examples.)
1. Describe two or three differences between "who you were" and "who you are now."
2. Explain why recovery is "a matter of the heart."

SHARE: (with your group or sponsor)
1. Tell about a time when you were the recipient of someone else's service work.
2. Tell about a time you were able to "carry the message" to a newcomer.

PRACTICE: Volunteer to help set up your meeting (set up chairs, make the coffee, and so on).

• • •

SECTION 7

Emotional Management

• **WEEK 26** •

Emotions and the Double Mind

Eight men sat around the table at their usual Saturday morning meeting. All were alcoholics or drug addicts. All were felons. None of them had more than a year clean and sober. But every one of them was committed to a new life in recovery. This was a topic meeting. The topic that day was "Pitfalls and Stumbles in Recovery."

Adam spoke first. He talked about his "double mind" and how closely he always had to pay attention to "that little hustler in my psychotic mind." He said that the previous week he'd driven through the "old hood" on his way home from church, of all places. As he got to the corner of the territory he once controlled, he said his "little hustler" started talking to him big time. Adam said in the blink of an eye, memories of all those "good times" and the "river of money" he'd once had on the street resurfaced and "made me feel like I was jumping out of my skin."

Turk said he knew just what his friend was talking about. "You ain't alone, brother," he said. "My double mind comes at me like a pack of wild dogs every day." Turk had lived under the heel of his addiction for forty-six years. About twenty-four of those years were spent in prison. Now he wants a clean and sober life. He really does. But, Turk says, "Everything seems to go so slow in recovery. Every day I feel like I need an excitement fix. I crave action."

Hector joined right in. "When things don't go my way, I feel like I'm going to unravel," he said. "I get frustrated easily and want to run out and get a forty-ounce bottle of beer and drink it as fast as I can—then see what comes next."

All of the men had similar stories. They all spoke of their "double mind"—the part that *wanted* recovery and the part that was always trying to pull them off their square.

Do you have some version of a double mind, or what Adam called a "psychotic mind"? In one way or another, everyone in recovery does. And the engine driving the dangerous part of that double mind is powered by the negative emotions associated with whatever triggers it.

Emotions run riot are tightly connected to relapse.

That's why emotional management is also tightly connected to sobriety and long-term recovery.

Ask someone what triggered a relapse, and the answer almost always has to do with a failure to manage emotions. Whatever the situation given as the cause, whatever the problem, when you lift the lid, you'll see an outbreak of "emotions run riot."

If you've ever relapsed, think back to the situation that triggered it. What emotion or emotions were involved? Do any of the following fit?

- anger
- boredom
- frustration
- resentments
- fear
- self-pity
- complacency
- loneliness
- guilt or shame
- need for excitement

Connect the emotions that cause you the most trouble to the dangerous voice of your double mind—and then to the urge to use again. Weren't these the emotions attached to the situation that tried to pull you off your square?

Understanding those connections is a central part of working your program. And as you learned in Week 4, problems don't cause relapse. What causes relapse is not working a strong enough program. Adam, Turk, and Hector *are* working an effective program (more detail on this in the following weeks) in that they *understand* (and therefore are not ambushed by) the feelings coming at them as they live their recovery.

Remember this: *Feelings and thoughts always occur together.* There is no such thing as a feeling without a thought, and no such thing as a thought without a feeling. And every thought and feeling we have registers in our bodies. In real lived life, thoughts, feelings, and bodily reactions all come together. To better understand who we are and how and why we make the decisions we do (especially those concerning relapse and recovery), we need to pull this unity apart and study the connections between them.

MAKE IT REAL

Answer the following questions in detail. Each week's lesson in this section on emotional management builds on the lessons in the previous week, so *please,* do not skip these questions or skimp on your efforts to answer them.

Write down a "trigger situation" that you struggle with in your recovery.

What emotion or emotions are attached to that situation? How do you best handle that situation? What works best for you in getting through that dangerous time?

Share your responses to these questions with the people you're working with, and then *listen* to their responses.

ACTION STEPS

Managing emotions is much easier said than done. But there are things you can do to make it less difficult and more effective. The program's advice to HALT (avoid getting too *hungry, angry, lonely,* or *tired*) is wise counsel. We all do better when we're fed and well rested!

WRITE: (two or three paragraphs if you can, on the following topics. Give personal examples.)
  1. Explain the connection between troubling emotions and relapse.
  2. What feelings come at you when your "double mind" is at work? Give examples.

SHARE: (with your group or sponsor)
1. Tell about people and places that, for you, present dangerous "trigger situations."
2. Describe two emotions that are hard for you to stay on top of.

CONSCIOUS CONTACT: In today's prayer and meditation, turn over your fears and resentments to your Higher Power.

• • •

• WEEK 27 •

Emotions Are Learned

Feelings, or emotions, are *learned*. Therefore, our feelings mostly reflect the feelings of our teachers. Now, isn't that an interesting thought?

Those three words—*emotions are learned*—hold an enormous amount of critical information for our recovery. They prompt us to ask some hard questions: If our feelings were learned, who were our teachers? What were the lessons? Do we still believe what we learned? And if we don't, what are we going to do about it?

Another important truth about feelings is that they are *habits*. As we all know, habits are the result of regular repetition. Once a habit is formed, it sinks into our subconscious, and from there we practice it thousands upon thousands of times during our lives. People don't necessarily need a reason to feel angry, less than, terrified, in danger, needy, guilty, betrayed, hopeless, and helpless. They just *always* feel that way. If you relate to this thought, here's the question: Is feeling this way a habit you need to change? Does it get in the way of your recovery? Does it affect the quality of your life?

Someone else taught us (then we practiced for all we were worth) what made us feel good or bad, right or wrong, acceptable or unacceptable, strong or weak, worthy or unworthy, a success or a failure. Whatever we learned back then became our unquestioned *truth*. Those ideas became *reality*. They dictated what we accepted as *normal*. Our emotions then formed a protective wall around that truth, reality, and normalcy. And they continue to protect their charges like snarling junkyard dogs.

But the lessons and the feelings that flow from our habitual reactions are all arbitrary! Because these lessons were based on opinions rather than facts, their validity is questionable. It depends on the teacher. Recovery demands we work to clarify the connection between what we were taught to feel and who did the teaching—and then determine if we still agree with those lessons.

READER ALERT: *There is an important lesson here. It is critical to spend the time and effort to learn it!*

As you were growing up, what were you taught about yourself? What feelings came with those lessons, or messages? Whether those messages were verbal or nonverbal, silent or screamed, delivered with a sneer or a doubled-up fist, do you recognize what they are? Do you see how they still operate in your life? Most important, do you agree with what they say about you?

What kind of messages might these be? Well, perhaps they sound something like this:

- You'll never amount to a damn!
- You are just like your mother/father/uncle/_____ (fill in the blank).
- You are too stupid to listen to.
- Your rights count less than nothing.
- You were a mistake from the start.
- Come over here, I want to hit you.
- Feelings are your enemy. Kill them.
- Lie to get by.
- If they have it and you want it, take it away from them.
- You are the only one who counts.
- Other _____

What was the main message your teachers taught you about yourself?

Pick one of the above examples you strongly relate to. Now, reflect on the *feelings* that stem from this lesson.

Here's the kicker: *Do you believe the lessons?* If the lessons are wrong, then the feelings attached and associated with them are also wrong. They are "wrong" because, once practiced, they became character defects (Week 25) that blocked spirituality (Week 14), which is the solution (Week 13) we now seek.

If you don't believe the lessons anymore, change is required. Anytime people go against the fundamental lessons they learned about themselves, there will be an emotional firestorm *until* a new lesson is practiced long enough for their emotions to line up with it (Week 14).

Recovery is all about learning to live by different values. As we practice these new values (by working the Steps—weeks 16 through 29), our feelings will realign themselves to support recovery behavior.

It doesn't happen all at once. Remember that recovery is a marathon, not a sprint. Remember Adam, Turk, and Hector in last week's work? They had to walk their way through a "blast of emotions" that would pull them back into active addiction if not understood, faced, and dealt with. And so does everyone else in recovery. *Everyone* in recovery has a double mind at times.

Recovery is not for the faint of heart. Knowing your story well enough to recognize these emotions and say, "I get it," is often the difference between making it and not making it. The emotional firestorms that occur in recovery, especially early recovery, are partly the result of the physical nature of the disease as well as our long-practiced self-defeating habits. *But those emotional firestorms can be weathered. They can be understood. You can make decisions to go against and through the firestorm.* Then you can start creating a new emotional foundation on which to build your new house of recovery.

Again, the lessons (values) you were taught and around which your emotions gathered are arbitrary. As children, we didn't know we had a choice. As adults, we do. What choice will you make about who others led you to believe you are, and what lengths are you willing to go in order to make that choice stick?

● ● ●

Jack had a year clean and sober. He was doing great. He went to meetings, studied the Big Book, did service work, and just about lived with his sponsor. His eyes were clear, and his face brimmed with joy and confidence. But then, little by little, he lost the miracle he was given. How?

Against his sponsor's advice to wait at least a year before starting a new relationship, he got involved with a woman. Jack said it was safe because she was in recovery. The woman was living in a facility with her three-year-old daughter. The rule of the house was no overnight guests. One evening, Jack wanted to stay the night. His girlfriend told him he couldn't because she wasn't going to risk losing this shelter for herself and her daughter.

Immediately, Jack's old, learned feelings of not being wanted, of being betrayed, of getting "thrown out" set on him like a pack of dogs. False pride kept him from calling his sponsor and asking for help. A few days later, when the police picked him up off the street, he was closer to dead than alive. His alcohol level was four times the legal limit.

Jack is still in detox. He says he's through trying to live a sober life and plans to get high as soon as he gets out. Who knows if he will get another chance at life or not? He failed by not fighting through the emotional firestorm and not separating his old, learned feelings from his present situation.

● ● ●

Molly on the other hand, six years clean and sober, has done the hard work of recovery. She used to be male dependent (the result of never feeling loved or cared about by her father or any other males in her family). Anytime Molly got around a man, her feelings told her, "Do *anything* for approval. Without male approval you don't exist." In the presence of a man, she felt panicky, scared, and excited all at the same time. Molly relapsed many, many times over not being able to sort out her feelings.

Now, when Molly feels scared and needy around men, she reframes her thoughts, claims the truth, and refuses to allow the feelings of the rejected little girl drive the bus of her adult life. Molly has surrounded herself with what she calls her "band of angels," five women from her larger group with whom she has shared her "screwed-up feelings." Anytime they see Molly slipping back into her "old stuff," they reach out and tell her to knock it off. They remind her of the truth of who she is *now*. These days, Molly is confident and sober, and she doesn't need a man's approval to feel okay.

M A K E   I T   R E A L

Emotions are tricky. Most of us use our feelings as the yardstick for judging what is right, good, or safe. But as we've seen in this week's work, *emotions can lie.* They don't lie about the past, but they sure do lie about the present. A major recovery skill is developing the ability to distinguish the feelings of "then" from "now." So *please,* do this work. It may well save your life.

As you were growing up, what message(s) did you receive about yourself? What emotions came from those lessons? Think about a concrete situation that triggered those emotions in your current life.

Explain the connection between the situation (the lesson involved) and the feelings that exploded around the event.

A C T I O N   S T E P S

If only our physical bodies were as enduring as our old ways of thinking and feeling! But as we grow in recovery, the differences between "then" and "now" become greater and greater. What no longer fits has got to go.

WRITE: (two or three paragraphs if you can, on the following topics. Give personal examples.)
1. What, according to your teachers, made you "good" or "bad"?
2. Explain why challenging our long-practiced emotional habits creates a "firestorm."

SHARE: (with your group or sponsor)
1. A lesson you were taught about yourself that you're no longer willing to accept.
2. One or two habitual feelings that you learned from your early teachers.

PRACTICE: When you find yourself on the brink of an emotional slide, say the Serenity Prayer:

God, grant me the serenity
To accept the things I cannot change,
The courage to change the things I can,
And the wisdom to know the difference.

● ● ●

• **WEEK 28** •

Emotional Management and Staying Connected

In Week 11, you learned the importance of staying connected. (You might want to revisit that week now to be sure you understand the relationship between staying connected and emotional management.) *All recovery is about staying connected.*

In Week 27, you learned that emotions are intimately tied to the messages we receive about ourselves and the values we internalize. And if those messages or lessons "lie"—if they do not tell us the truth about ourselves in a basic spiritual sense—then so do the feelings connected to them. The lessons lie if they say we are stupid, unworthy, a mistake, or any of the other negative characterizations listed in Week 27. The resulting feelings lie because they attach us to that toxic, tragic, and untrue message—and they lead us in exactly the opposite direction of spiritual living (weeks 11 through 15).

A key point in last week's work was that "anytime people go against the fundamental lessons they learned about themselves, there will be an emotional firestorm."

If the lessons we were taught and practiced and internalized about ourselves block the development of honest, humble, and loving connections with our Higher Power, self, and others, then the emotions accompanying those lessons will also block these crucial spiritual connections. Again, I can't stress strongly enough how much it helps to *understand* where the feelings are coming from and what lessons they are attached to.

In recovery, we finally challenge those messages about ourselves and work to let go of feelings connected to the messages we no longer buy. As we rebuild our lives, we develop new skills and live new values that support our connections with the God of our understanding, self, and others. Five of the key values are

- honesty
- trust
- commitment
- caring
- responsibility

These recovery values are the foundation and bedrock of all healthy connections. (Later, we will see the same values as essential to the functioning of all healthy relationships.)

The simple (but far from easy) work for this week is to take a rigorously honest look at each of these values by writing out the following for yourself:

1. This is what I was taught (verbal, nonverbal, silent, physical, and so on) about how *each* of these values relates to me.
2. These emotions are triggered whenever I get close to a behavior involving *each* of these values.
3. Describe a specific situation where your emotions were triggered by *each* of the five values.

I know very well how easily these exercises can become intellectual head games. I know from experience that many people in new (or new again) recovery are so full of guilt and shame, so full of grief and self-loathing, so full of doubt and self-blame or ego and pride, that completing these exercises seems beyond them. *I understand.*

But I also understand that *not* working through such exercises dramatically raises the risk that we'll fall back into active addiction. Above all, people living under the boot heel of crippling guilt or pride need the connection to their Higher Power, self, and others. They need the power of these connections flowing through the Fellowship.

Of course, many who attempt to form those honest, trusting, loving connections—which requires using the five skills or values listed—will be met with *intense* emotional resistance, not because what they are trying to accomplish is wrong, but simply because they have learned that they have no right to anything so grand and good as what happens in recovery. They don't trust what they are being asked to do. Past attempts, often starting in childhood, always left them broken and bloody. And that is what the accustomed feelings remember—*broken and bloody*.

Feelings face backward. Feelings only know what *was*. And what *was*, was active addiction and all the misery that comes with it (Week 4). Many (if not most) of us already have a Ph.D. in guilt, shame, self-contempt, anger, rage, frustration, and "denied access" to the soft hand of love that every heart craves from birth.

We fear that recovery—opening up to fellowship, community, trust, and faith—will surely lead only to more suffering and betrayal, which our emotions remember only too well.

To set foot firmly on the new road of recovery requires recognizing the role that emotions play in our lives, where they come from, and what they tell us. Most of all, it requires understanding where these emotions *always* lead us.

But "now" is not "then." Recovery offers a choice. It is a choice that must be rigorously exercised even in the face of fear, risk, and a certain amount of pain. (But what significant achievement doesn't require as much?) And the payoff in this case—recovery—towers above all others. It is rising from the dead. The glory of recovery rises as high as the dismal darkness of active addiction took us down. And it is *possible*. It is a choice. The choice is to stay connected or fall away (Week 11).

I'm speaking to you, the ones struggling the most with this work, the ones most trapped in the dark room of fear, guilt, and shame—to you above all, no matter what your situation. *I urge you to put hand to plow and to stand up for yourself, for all who love you, and for those who will come after you.* I urge you to make the effort and tap into the power not of this earth that is met through the Fellowship. *Stay the course.* People more damaged than you have made it. People less damaged than you have not. The degree of damage is not at issue. The only thing at issue is our willingness to be honest, open, and willing.

MAKE IT REAL

The work for this week is clearly set forth in the previous pages. *Please do the work. Your recovery is worth it.*

Then share what you've learned. Listen as others share what they have learned. Support each other in getting through an emotional firestorm—as Adam, Turk, and Hector did.

ACTION STEPS

We're *not* doomed! Our accustomed emotional responses can change by making different choices. As we foster our vital connections with the God of our understanding, self, and others, "the way we were" gives way to a new life that's better than we can even imagine.

WRITE: (two or three paragraphs if you can, on the following topics. Give personal examples.)
1. Explain the relationship between false pride and honesty. Give an example from your own life.
2. Drawing on your own life, write about a time that misplaced trust left you "broken and bloody."

SHARE: (with your group or sponsor)
1. Make a commitment to your group that you will "keep coming back," no matter how you feel.
2. Tell about a positive action you've taken "in the face of fear."

CONSCIOUS CONTACT: Thank your Higher Power for the opportunity to take control of your own emotions.

• • •

• **WEEK 29** •

Facing Up to Fear

The Big Book says that resentments are the number one cause of relapse. The founders, of course, knew of what they spoke. I wonder if they would agree that *fear* is the next biggest cause?

Many would say no—ego is the next biggest cause of relapse. Maybe so.

But it is my experience that much of what passes for ego and pride is really fear wearing a mask. Most people I've met along the way don't so much think they're superior to others. In truth, they fear they are not as good as others, so they go to extremes to convince themselves and everyone else of their worth. Yearning for approval and acceptance, they tend to act badly when they're afraid they won't ever be considered worthy.

Fear is at the bottom of most expressions of our character defects. Fear blocks connections and thus spirituality—which is the only solution to addiction (weeks 21 through 25). That's why this week's lesson is devoted to fear.

A definition of fear: The emotional response to perceived danger. Danger triggers fear. The more imminent the danger, the greater and more fierce the fear. Danger can be deadly. Danger predicts misery and pain if we don't protect ourselves or get out of its way.

But fear itself isn't the enemy. Some fear is necessary for survival. If the ice is cracking under our feet, we'd better be afraid and *get off the ice* as quickly as we can. Fear saves lives.

The problem is about what we have learned to be afraid of. What kinds of situations trigger an alarm if we approach?

Managing our emotions means coming to *understand* and then to *recognize* what the fear is attached to and then making adjustments if necessary. What is our fear telling us? Many of us have learned to hear the ice cracking even when we are standing in the middle of a desert. In other words, we may be experiencing fear when we're not in any danger. In recovery, the presence of fear may also signify our discomfort at making healthy changes. It often tells us that we are right where we should be and that we need to "press on," to keep going *even in the face of fear*, to have courage (Week 20). Why? Because on the other side of that fear is the land of the Promises.

Of course, like everything else in recovery, this work requires that we stay connected. Yet our connections with others are just what many are afraid of—what many have found to be so dangerous. And for good reason.

Nothing hurts more than trusting and then having that trust betrayed. Nothing wounds deeper than reaching out for that "soft hand of love"—especially in our formative years—but instead receiving messages that harmed our spirit, lies such as "You don't count. You aren't worthy. You aren't enough." As the tree is bent, so shall it grow.

Rather than the "soft hand of love," what many of us got was a fist in the face or at best a cold shoulder. Not everyone, surely not everyone. But many. Those who had a better start and then "crossed the line" into active addiction learned their spiritual lies of self-contempt as they spiraled down.

Either way, whether from the start or later on, everyone with an active addiction comes to recovery with a fear of intimacy. This fear is behind our avoidance of honesty, trust, closeness, and connection. If we have also been saddled with the effects of childhood abuse or a form of dual diagnosis, gathering the courage to reach out to others may be just that much more difficult.

Yet difficult or not, the journey must—and can—be made.

We need to do what we most fear; we need to strive for what eluded us in the past—honesty, trust, commitment, caring, and responsibility. Every active addict has practiced and is a master at slipping around these dangerous corners. (It was once said in a meeting of an especially slippery person that he "lived in a round building so he couldn't get caught in any corners.")

Do you want to hear testimony to the insanity of the disease (Week 10)? The same person who is absolutely terrified of the "danger of Fellowship" will run like an Olympic sprinter back to situations that stole every speck of what makes life worthwhile (Week 4).

Understanding the lessons on emotional management (Section 7 of this book) can be a huge help in not falling victim to a firestorm of fear. Once you learn how feelings work, you'll be much better able to "call fear's bluff" and not get pulled off the road.

Here are some of the typical ways we run from fear: (1) withdrawing, (2) isolating, (3) eating, (4) blaming, (5) spending, (6) working to exhaustion, (7) fighting, (8) switching addictions, and the obvious, (9) using again. Rather than immediately and blindly reacting to fear, we must practice better ways of dealing with it.

It's not easy to stand in the face of fear and say, "Wait a minute. I recognize what you are and where you come from. But I also understand that to recover I need to get past you. I need to act. I need to open up to myself and my group. I need to tell the truth. I need to be honest. I need to own the damage I've done to myself and others— and ask forgiveness. And beyond forgiveness, I need to make amends in the manner taught by my program. I must put myself on the line for others. I *must* be of service."

No, it's not easy, but it is doable. There is no task that willing human beings in connection with the God of their understanding and the Fellowship cannot accomplish. Nothing is stronger than a spiritually fortified and connected human being.

Feel the fear. Then question it. Listen to what it is telling you. Then decide what is best for you to do—regardless of how you feel.

MAKE IT REAL

1. Sit down at the table with your fear. Look it in the face. Reflect on what you are afraid of and why. Then write your fear a letter. Tell it who you are *now* and how you are going to deal with it in the future. Set out your guidelines for handling fear.
2. Then, as always, share your work with your trusted others.

3. Finally, write out for yourself what you've learned from this work. What was the lesson in all of this for you?

A C T I O N   S T E P S

Why do so many of us hate to admit fear? Because doing so makes us feel weak, childish, cowardly. That's why we slap masks on our fears and call them by other names. But fear (whether of failure, rejection, closeness, or something else) is the master of all negative emotions. Our delivery from hopelessness depends on our willingness to be brave enough to face our fear.

WRITE: (two or three paragraphs if you can, on the following topics. Give personal examples.)
1. For you, what has been a typical tactic (denial or isolation, for example) for running away from your fears?
2. What resources do you have to help you fight your fears? Describe two or three.

SHARE: (with your group or sponsor)
1. Tell about one or two situations that have always triggered your fears.
2. Tell about a time you confronted fear and kept right on going.

CONSCIOUS CONTACT: Turn over your fears to the care of your Higher Power. (Name your fears specifically.)

● ● ●

• WEEK 30 •

Four-Step Emotional Management Strategy

The four weeks in this section are loaded with work. Managing emotions is a big job. It takes time and a *lot* of attention to hear the voices in your double mind, to recognize whose voices they are and what they are telling you, and to decide whether or not you believe what they are saying.

Here's a four-step process for doing the work of emotional management. The four steps are UNDERSTAND, STOP, SEEK OPTIONS, ACT. Each step has a dynamic place in the practice of emotional management.

All emotions, whatever their differences, operate the same way. The same steps apply whether you're learning to manage anger, lust, rage, ego, guilt, shame, fear, or any other emotion. Management is management.

Run your story through these four steps and judge for yourself. Share your insights with others and listen to their input. What does it all boil down to?

UNDERSTAND

By UNDERSTAND, I mean "think through" the work you've done from Week 1 onward. Gaining self-knowledge is the first step toward taking charge of your emotions. Remember that we all *learn* our feelings.

What did you learn? Who did the teaching? What brokenness or bias did your teachers bring with them into the classroom of your life? Whose voice is speaking to you through your double mind—that of the child you were or the adult you are? What "old normal" is being poured into your consciousness by your emotions? What are the consequences? If you don't want the box of TNT to blow up, don't light the fuse. Don't start. What emotion, in what situation, is lighting that fuse for you?

Do these questions seem terribly daunting or complicated? If you break up the work into the "bites" suggested in the preceding weeks, the answers will slowly reveal themselves. If they don't, take a break. Go back and do or review your work from the past three weeks.

The only "wrong" answer is "I'm not smart enough to do this work. It's too hard." Yes, you can. *All the questions above simply ask you to know your own story.* Look at your life. Recognize what you see. If you won't take responsibility to know your own life and take charge of it, who will? Whose job is it if not yours?

STOP

STOP simply means *stop*. When an emotion reaches out to take the driver's wheel of your life—stop. Feelings must not be allowed to dictate our behavior. Feelings only know what *was*. They face backward and aren't trustworthy guides into the future. All too often, our feelings are attached to old, self-destructive beliefs, values, and lessons from yesterday. Recovery demands that we challenge and examine those feelings through the lens of understanding *before* we give them access to the gas pedal.

Pay attention. Know where the feeling is taking you.

Sometimes feelings pounce on us in full-storm force, as happened with Adam back in Week 26. That's called "stimulus control." Get anywhere near the people, places, or things that were part of the drinking or drugging experience, and the fuse is lit. As well as an emotional and mental response, there's often a physical response, such as sweating, shivering, rapid heartbeat, quickened pulse—it's all there. BAM. Now what?

Without building and practicing a system to handle such occasions, there's no space between the impulse and the act. *Feel it* equals *do it*. But with practice and a powerful support system in place, you can create a space between the impulse and the act. You might call it a built-in "pause button" that allows you to stop before being kidnapped by emotions run riot.

Many of us new to recovery have groaned and said things like, "Can't happen! This is too hard. You don't know *my* story. I have a birth defect. I was born without a 'pause' button. I know I can't do this. I just can't learn to stop."

But many who started this way did learn. They disciplined themselves up front so they didn't have to pay the bill of regret later. That's the choice: discipline or regret—the price of Week 4 or the Promises of Week 15.

Those who did learn through paying attention and practice, like Turk and Hector in Week 26, were able to stand up and help their friend Adam through the firestorm that jumped him on his old street. And Adam, if he is willing, will learn to stop. Then he will be able to bear witness that no matter what, feelings do *not* automatically have the power to throw people off their chosen road of recovery.

SEEK OPTIONS

Choice is all about OPTIONS. Of course, you can't make a choice unless you have options to choose from. If all you know is road A, there is no chance of traveling road B (because you don't know there's a road B).

Feelings don't offer options. They know nothing about choices. Feelings can only do one thing: protect and support what *was*. They serve yesterday's king because that's all they know.

One of the most powerful spiritual awakenings is to realize that *you do have a choice*. It is to grasp, in total amazement, that "just because I've always been this way" doesn't mean "I always *have* to be this way."

Profoundly selfish, self-centered people *can* grow to the point where, if they pay attention and practice, other people matter, too— no matter what their feelings tell them.

Terrified, passive people *can* grow to the point where, if they pay attention and practice, they can stand their ground rather than run away—no matter what their feelings tell them.

Truly male- or female-dependent people *can* grow to the point where, if they pay attention and practice, they feel okay without constant outside validation from a male or female source—no matter what their feelings tell them.

Habitually angry people *can* grow to the point where, if they pay attention and practice, they realize that *not* everyone, everywhere is their enemy—no matter what their feelings tell them.

Slippery secret-keepers *can* learn, if they pay attention and practice, to tell the truth without deletions, edits, and spin—no matter what their feelings tell them.

People riddled by self-contempt and self-criticism *can* learn, if they pay attention and practice, to hear the uncertain music of self-compassion rising from deep within—no matter what their feelings tell them.

Materialists who find security only in things *can* learn, if they pay attention and practice, to value the riches of the spirit more than anything that can be bought—no matter what their feelings tell them.

Loners who fear connections like a dread disease *can* learn, if they pay attention and practice step by step, to willingly give others access to their lives—no matter what their feelings tell them.

Which one of these examples best fits you? Write down your thoughts—they are the groundwork for what follows.

There are options in any situation. The price of emotional management is to STOP long enough—before rushing into action—to consider what those options might be. Refuse to allow yourself to be limited to only road A. Road A may well be a one-way route to relapse.

ACT

Once you see an option, road B, practice taking it. Every time you make a life-affirming, recovery-affirming choice, you strengthen your ability to choose that option again. Feelings follow actions. If you want to change your feelings, you need to change your actions—then keep repeating the new action until behaving self-compassionately feels as normal as acting self-destructively.

ACT. Only doing is doing. And by and by, mostly without our

even being aware of it, we will find that we have changed. Step by step we will move away from the isolation of spiritual bankruptcy and create connections our old feelings would never have allowed.

Then, amazingly, by way of a spiritual awakening, a moment of clarity, it dawns on us that that old way is as offensive and unacceptable as our new way is life-affirming and comfortable. It's the way "I choose to be."

Not that a stray bolt of emotional energy from the past may not come pounding on our door from time to time. That's just life. But once we've learned not to be intimidated by a negative emotion, it simmers down to "no big deal." We work a little recovery magic on it by using the tools in our familiar toolbox, and it fades away. We "get it" at last: Just because something pounds on our door doesn't mean we have to open it. We choose whether or not to open that door. It's an option we are absolutely free to take—or not.

MAKE IT REAL

The work for this week is to apply each of the four steps for developing emotional management to your life. Give an example of how each of these steps fit (or could fit) with your recovery. Hint: Always start with a specific. Traction is impossible with generalities. We're after traction.

A specific troublesome emotion that I choose to manage better is

_____.

Understand: Review the model of work offered in Week 28. Use the emotion you just listed as the place to start in this model.

Stop: Describe a *concrete situation* in your life where your normal response was to immediately swing into action because of the rush of emotion. Explain the situation in detail. Who was there? What was said? What happened? What did you feel? What were the consequences?

Seek options: In *that* concrete situation, no matter how unrealistic or awkward it seems now, what were your options? Other than doing what you did, what could you have done? What would those consequences have likely been?

Act: In *that* situation, how *might* you have acted? What could you have done instead? In a similar situation (because a similar situation is just around the corner waiting to jump you again), how will you choose to act?

It's best to internalize these steps until doing them becomes as natural as breathing. Practice. Practice. Practice. Sometimes slowly and sometimes with a leap, those who pay the price of practice come to a clear awareness: "Oh my God! I *do* have a choice. I don't have to let my emotions run my life." *Then* doesn't always have to be *now*. It's a beautiful thing to see this realization, this giant step along the road of recovery, come into clear focus.

The ability to keep internalizing these steps, however, long after you've worked your way through this book, depends on *using your tools*. If you don't keep using your recovery tools, the light fades. You start to forget (weeks 4 through 7). You easily become isolated, and then, cut off from the strength of your connections, you become easy prey for your addiction.

ACTION STEPS

Knee-jerk, out-of-control emotions are ruinous to our relationships with others—as well as to our own serenity. We have everything to gain and nothing to lose by doing this work.

WRITE: (two or three paragraphs if you can, on the following topics. Give personal examples.)
1. Give two or three reasons why better emotional management is in your own best interest.
2. Tell about a time when *you* were negatively affected by someone else's emotional outburst.

SHARE: (with your group or sponsor)
1, Any doubts you have about your ability to "put a lid on" an emotion run riot.
2. An example of your most troubling emotional pattern. (What

situation provoked this emotion? How did you express it? How did you feel afterward?)

CONSCIOUS CONTACT: Every day this week, ask your Higher Power to replace your negative emotions with gratitude and love.

PRACTICE: Lighten up! Enjoy the sunshine. Listen to happy music. Give someone a compliment or a pat on the back.

● ● ●

The Toolkit

• WEEK 31 •

The Right Tool for the Right Job

Like his father before him, my father was a plasterer. As such, he figured he was kin to Michelangelo, since the Renaissance master often worked his magic in wet plaster. They were both artists, Dad thought. One of his favorite sayings was "A man has to have the right tool for the right job."

It's true that a plasterer needs the right tool to plaster in tight places. The right tools are also critical when creating a life of deep and lasting recovery—life's greatest art.

Or look at it this way—having dreams and setting goals are certainly worthy uses of energy. But our goals are only as good as the *plans we make* for turning them into realities. Goals without plans are mere wishes. They have no depth or legs. Wishes are washed away by the tide like yesterday's footprints on the beach.

A person's goal to run a marathon is only viable if he or she is willing to START TRAINING and build up to running that distance.

A goal to improve one's education is only viable if that person is willing to find out where the right schooling is available and then FOLLOW UP by taking the classes.

Is your goal to learn a second language? That goal is only viable if you're willing to PRACTICE that language until you become fluent.

You get the idea—any goal worth achieving requires effort. That is why I have repeatedly insisted that you do the work prescribed in this book.

Recovery is as high a calling as a human being can have. Echoing the founders, "A life of recovery is a spiritual life." There's nothing a human being can do that's more important or more noble than practicing a spiritual life. An authentic spiritual life breathes through its connection with our Higher Power, self, and others. And those connections only endure if we're willing to do small things, the everyday acts that keep them alive and strong. Every one of the past fifteen weeks focused on doing one small thing—the next right thing—that creates the spiritual condition upon which our "twenty-four-hour reprieve" is won. Each one of the attitudes (weeks 16 through 20), the Steps (weeks 21 through 25), and the elements of emotional management (weeks 26 through 30) are spiritual luminaries. Each one leads us from the bitterness of our winter night to the warm welcome of our homecoming. The work we did in each of these fifteen weeks lights the way as we continue to go forward.

So now we know what "the next right thing" is, but how do we *keep doing* the work? Where do we get the strength? How do we—people who once ran away from honesty, trust, and responsibility—endure in doing "the next right thing" of recovery? How do we go on taking enough "next steps" to reach the end of our race?

The answer is that we *learn to use the tools in our toolkit.* The right tools keep us connected. And staying connected takes us all the way home, one day at a time.

At different times along the way, we need different tools. Sometimes what gets the job done is getting out of self by reaching out to others in need. Sometimes what works is sitting down and studying the Big Book. Sometimes it's having a good heart-to-heart talk with our sponsor. Sometimes it's getting on our knees in an Eleventh Step and seeking the God of our understanding through prayer and meditation. And always, always, always, it's staying connected to the Fellowship. It's not just going to a meeting, but going to a meeting *with our ears and hearts open.* It's being honest, open, and willing to reveal whatever is going on inside of us. No secrets. It's *telling on our addiction.*

In the following weeks, we will discuss eight tools often mentioned in the program. We'll find out how using these eight tools keeps us connected—which is the sweet spot of all recovery (Week 11).

The eight tools in our recovery toolkit that we'll explore are the following:

- practicing spirituality
- getting a sponsor
- going to meetings/group
- doing service work
- working the Steps
- studying the Big Book
- practicing gratitude
- having fun

Remember that at different times in our recovery, different tools become more important—at that moment, they are "the right tool for the right job." The trick is to pay attention to what's happening *right now* in our own lives so we'll have the proper tool at hand when the need arises. The good news is that building this toolbox is a do-able task. Piece by piece, we can put it together, and we already have a good start!

MAKE IT REAL

List three "rough spots" you passed through in your recovery during the last six months. Write them out. What was going on? Who else was involved? What specific form of stinking thinking ran through your head? How did you feel?

What got you through those times? What tool did you use (even if you never thought of your responses as tools)? At those times, what worked for you to keep you connected and on course?

What was the lesson? When you used the right tool for the right job, what did you learn that you can use again when it is needed?

As always, *please,* do the work. Answer these questions as fully and in as much detail as you can. Share your work with others. Listen to *their* experiences. Somewhere down the line, you will need the wisdom that develops through answering and sharing these questions.

ACTION STEPS

Using appropriate tools only makes sense. Can you imagine being reluctant to use a jack when you've got a flat tire? How blessed we are that those who have gone before us created such a wonderful toolkit!

WRITE: (two or three paragraphs if you can, on the following topics. Give personal examples.)
1. Suppose you're tired and frustrated about a problem at work or a disagreement with your spouse. Write about two "tools" that could help you.
2. On your way to a meeting, how could you prepare yourself to "open your mind and heart"? Give two or three ideas.

SHARE: (with your group or sponsor)
1. Tell about something you read in the Big Book that was especially helpful to you.
2. What was the last Step you worked? Explain the circumstances.

CONSCIOUS CONTACT: Say the Tenth Step aloud before going to sleep at night.

REACH OUT: Identify a friend in the program who's also learning how to use his or her "toolkit." Arrange to keep in touch by phone to share your mutual progress.

• • •

• WEEK 32 •

Practicing Spirituality

Our Third Step says that we "Made a decision to turn our will and our lives over to the care of God *as we understood Him.*"

That Step is wise counsel for everyone. But the Steps were not directed at *everyone.* They were crafted specifically for good men and women suffering devastating addiction brought on by a physical predisposition in conjunction with an ever-worsening state of spiritual bankruptcy.

Spiritual bankruptcy is both the cause and the consequence of isolation. And being totally isolated, the *last* thing addicts are willing or prepared to do is surrender their lives to anything or anyone—especially to the "care" of any agent outside of self.

"Care" means trust. It means trusting that someone, anyone—especially the One—would or could actually care for them, who have cared so little for themselves for such a long, long time. Only those coming from this state of spiritual bankruptcy can grasp the unimaginable leap it is to "turn one's life over" and trust that they are cared for. Only those who have fallen so far and walked in such total darkness can comprehend both the absolute blessing *and* the paralyzing terror of practicing the deep spirituality that recovery is and the demands of those who would join the Fellowship.

Getting clean and sober is the easy part. Learning to love yourself and others is what brings on the bloody sweat. We all have a double mind: With our right hand we reach for recovery while our left reaches back for the disaster of using again. "Want to" is not the same as "able to." Knowing isn't doing. Only doing is doing. And that is where our double mind trips us up (Week 26).

We know we need to turn to our Higher Power. But where do we most need that power and what exactly do we need it for? In recovery, spirituality means taking that power down to the X, the point where our double mind starts to kick in. We see the box of TNT in front of us. We see the fuse leading to the TNT. It's obvious that if you don't want the TNT to blow up, you don't light the fuse. When the fire hits the TNT, it's too late to duck.

Even though you don't *want* the blowup, it takes a power "not of this earth," a "Power greater than ourselves" to stay away from the fuse. It takes our Higher Power to keep us sober.

I'm not talking theory here or just mouthing high-sounding words. What I'm saying is *spirituality must matter—and that means doing something different before the match meets the fuse.* That means getting and staying connected with the God of your understanding so you don't relapse into your former life of despair.

Spirituality that isn't deep, that doesn't go through our humanity, amounts to nothing but smoke and mirrors. It's nothing but pose and game playing. It's powerless when we're faced with the toughest decisions, those that have the potential to destroy all we've worked for. *Do not light the fuse!*

Have you taken your Higher Power, the God of your understanding, to *that* place? To that inner place where you store your deepest secrets, struggles, and doubts? Have you invited your Higher Power to that place where we've exhaustively trained ourselves to hit, hide, or run whenever we see authentic intimacy come walking toward us?

For spirituality to make a difference, it *must* matter. It must have the power to *do something.* Our Higher Power can help us stay honestly and humbly connected—and endure in the program—in the face of all the other forces that would hold us back and drag us down. But in order to receive this support and strength, we must open ourselves to that power.

Most particularly, we must invite our Higher Power into the darkest corner of our fear. We must say, "Come! You are welcome here." We must act, "Come! You are welcome here." We must plead like our lives depend on it (because they do), "Come! You are welcome here."

Practicing spirituality means being connected to your Higher Power, self, and others. It means abandoning our lives of isolation and embracing lives of connection. Different people discover their value and worth through the lifeblood of connection in different ways. Consider this example:

• • •

I took my car to the garage to be serviced. While waiting, I was shown to the lounge, where coffee and donuts were laid out. It looked like an ordinary enough scene, but you never know when you'll see an angel.

The lounge was roughly horseshoe-shaped around a TV. There were eight or nine men waiting there. They all appeared bored and impatient. None of the men looked at each other, none talked, and each guy seemed intent on silently communicating to everyone else, "Don't bother me. I can take care of myself. I don't need company."

One man, however, who I'd guess was in his late seventies, was tired-looking and seemed nervous. His cane and slightly shaking hand suggested that he'd had some health problems. Just as I entered, he kicked over his can of soda. With considerable effort, he planted his cane and rose out of his chair. Cussing softly, he looked around helplessly. Enough of the soda had spilled that there was a large puddle under his chair. He could hardly ignore the mess, but what could he do? He was clearly embarrassed in front of the other men. His look reminded me of a schoolboy who'd wet his pants.

A man at the top of the horseshoe was someone I recognized from a meeting. Today, he looked like the most macho and defiant guy imaginable. The guy was a biker with a past as rough and rugged as he looked. He wore a do-rag with an eagle and stars over his head, reflective shades that hid his eyes, and a leather vest with some kind of insignia on it. He wasn't actually physically big, but he projected a big presence. And the expression on his face was far from friendly. Every man in the room was aware of him, no matter how indifferent to each other they appeared to be.

Then this alpha dog hopped up and grabbed a handful of napkins off the coffee table. He walked over to the sputtering, helpless older man, got down on his knees, and spread out the napkins to soak up the spill. The job took maybe thirty seconds. When he finished scooping up the soaking napkins, he chuckled and said to the old man, "Hell, if this is the worst thing that happens to us today, we'll be lucky."

No big deal. He threw the soggy napkins in the trash can and sat back down in his chair—once again retreating to his ultra-cool demeanor.

My path and that biker's had crossed several times. I knew him well enough to be amused, so I sat down next to him and asked, "What are you doing? You've got every guy in here looking sidewise at you. They think you're some kind of psychotic thug. Why are you playing tough guy?"

He gave me a huge smile and said, "I'm just clowning, having some fun. But I couldn't let that old guy stay in the mess he was in. That's in one of the Steps, isn't it?"

"It's in *all* of them," I told him. When he got up to leave, he said, "See you at group Saturday." I said, "Yes, you will." The name of our group is the Junkyard Dogs. But, that day, to the embarrassed older man, his rescuer was more of an angel.

MAKE IT REAL

Have you identified that place where your deepest fears and doubts live? Are you clear about where the "fuse" is that can blow up the box of TNT in no time at all? Do you know exactly where inside yourself you must take the God of your understanding?

ACTION STEPS

What do "program people" mean when they talk about spirituality? They're talking about life as it could be and should be—not just the opposite of death, but life in all its fullness. Impossible, you say? Not if you ask for help and then *take action.*

WRITE: (two or three paragraphs if you can, on the following topics. Give personal examples.)
1. Describe the "darkest corner of your fear" that is most in need of spiritual healing.
2. Explain why you think trust is so difficult for many addicts.

SHARE: (with your group or sponsor)
1. Explain what your Higher Power does for you that you cannot do for yourself.
2. Describe two habitual thoughts or behaviors that keep you isolated.

CONSCIOUS CONTACT: Ask your Higher Power for the courage to open your mind and your heart to your full human potential.

• • •

• WEEK 33 •

On Getting and Using a Sponsor

There is no one right way to be a sponsor. Sponsoring is as much a matter of style as anything else. A style that works for one person might not be right for another. At certain stages of our recovery, we may well need a style of help that wouldn't be fitting at a different time.

Some sponsors have a dozen or more sponsees. Working with so many people, sponsors using this style basically take a "Call me if you have a problem and we'll talk about it" approach. Some sponsors with many fewer people under their wing make a contract with their sponsees to commit to a phone call every day. This style obviously centers around daily contact. Other sponsors, with even fewer sponsees than the "call every day" folks, insist that their sponsees go through the Big Book or a Step class with them. This style is intense and can be very demanding.

The point is that one size *doesn't* fit all. It's important to know what you need and then go find the style of sponsorship that will be most helpful in your recovery.

You might be thrown off by hearing a phrase such as "know what you need." That instruction leaves many newly recovering people blank. A typical response is something like, "How do *I* know what I need? I'm new at this. Look where my best thinking got me so far. I don't know what I need!"

Here's a good rule of thumb: Keep your eyes and ears open. *Look for someone along the way whose recovery you admire.* Find someone who works his or her recovery in a way that you not only admire but know deep in your heart you need to practice yourself. That person is a good candidate to be your sponsor.

For decades I've used this analogy—find someone who has a light-bulb on his or her hat. You'll know it when you see it. Their heart will speak to your heart. You'll know.

Here's an example of how it works: It just so happened that James's sobriety birthday and real birthday are on the same day. So on his first sober birthday and forty-fourth biological birthday, James threw a party. He fancied himself one of the world's best barbecue grillers. (As it turned out, he wasn't far off!)

During the feast, James made a comment about a bad deal he got from one of the other group members, who'd referred him for a lawn care job. James did the work, but was paid only a fraction of what he was promised.

James's sponsor (who was at the party) immediately spoke up and told James he had to talk to this man. He explained he couldn't afford to carry a resentment around with him. No two ways about it. So right then and there, they made a plan for when and how James was going to set up an "honest face-to-face" with the brother in recovery.

That's what staying connected with a sponsor means. It means establishing a pipeline of honesty and trust through which the spirituality of the program can flow. What you do with a sponsor is PRACTICE! *It's all about practice.* It's about getting over to the right side of the goalpost (Week 13) and staying there.

• • •

Take Lonny, for example. Lonny has nearly five years clean and sober after a terribly rough start. One of the deep, dark, secret fires of rage and resentment burning in his spiritual belly was over the murder of his three-year-old son. One day, Lonny and his wife had dropped their son off at a reputable day care service before they went to work. A few hours later, one of the day care workers shook the child so severely he died. (That day care worker eventually was sentenced to life with the possibility of parole.)

Although he'd never done prison time himself, Lonny and his sponsor developed a routine of regularly taking the program into prisons. Lonny found this form of carrying the message deeply satisfying. On one of their prison visits, Lonny met up with John. John had been convicted of murdering two men in a drug deal gone bad and was doing life with the possibility of parole (although he had been repeatedly denied parole). When Lonny met him, John had already served twenty-five years in prison.

As it happened, Lonny and John became friends. They began exchanging letters. Frequently, Lonny returned to the prison to visit John, even when there wasn't a meeting scheduled. When it came to his new friend John, Lonny often said, "People can change" and "Forgiveness is the first step of healing." That's all it took for Lonny's sponsor to step in.

"What about you forgiving the woman who killed your baby?" his sponsor asked him. "She didn't do anything your friend John didn't do! Why are you all about forgiveness when it comes to John and yet you still hang on to the horrible resentment you still have for this woman?"

Of course, Lonny didn't want to hear that. He fought it. He was sure that it wasn't the same thing at all. But his sponsor continued to hold his feet to the fire of truth and honesty. "The only difference is that one crime happened to you and the other happened to someone else. Do what you want," his sponsor went on, "but remember this: You will only be forgiven as far as you are willing to forgive others."

As it turned out, Lonny did make amends to this woman (who was still in prison after serving fourteen years). He apologized for carrying around so much hate and venom toward her for all those years. Instead of demanding that she seek *his* forgiveness, Lonny came around a huge spiritual bend. He had now become ready to ask the woman's forgiveness for himself.

MAKE IT REAL

This necessary step in Lonny's recovery never would have happened without his trusted, beloved sponsor. Who points out necessary steps that *you* need to take to keep progressing in recovery?

A special note to any and all reading this who feel a clutch in the stomach, a throbbing just behind the eyes, a wave (maybe a tidal wave) of resistance at just the *thought* of actually asking someone to be your sponsor. The more resistance you feel about finding a sponsor, the more you need to practice courage (Week 20). Press on through to *do it.* Use the connection of your spirituality by taking your Higher Power where it matters—into the dark room of your deepest fear. If your Higher Power brought you *to* this point, your Higher Power will also take you *through* it. Your Higher Power will take you through your fears of honesty, trust, and self-revelation to the life that awaits you—a life at the heart of the Promises.

ACTION STEPS

Are you ready and willing to make some real progress in the program? Nothing will be more helpful than the personal counsel of a wise sponsor. So get serious about finding someone who meets your needs. Ask for his or her help. Get it done.

WRITE: (two or three paragraphs if you can, on the following topics. Give personal examples.)

If you don't yet have a sponsor:
1. List the qualities and attitudes you most need in a sponsor.
2. If you can, list three people who would meet your needs. If you can't, list three places you might meet such people.

If you already have a sponsor:
1. Is there a secret or troubling area that you have not yet shared with your sponsor? What is it?
2. How might your sponsor help you do specific work around that hidden secret or character defect?

SHARE: (with your group or sponsor)
1. Ask members of your group, "How did you first approach *your* sponsor?"
2. Tell your group about any hesitance or fear you have about asking someone to sponsor you. Ask for their advice.

CONSCIOUS CONTACT: Thank your Higher Power for the chance to renew your life through the Fellowship.

• • •

• WEEK 34 •

Going to Group

Why is regularly going to group so essential for recovery? (If the answer doesn't immediately come to mind, review weeks 11 through 15 for an outline of the exact nature of the solution.)

We've already discussed how to develop the skills necessary to find the solution—connection. It's all about practice and repetition (Week 1). So the questions must be asked: *Practice where? Practice how? Practice what?*

The answer is: That's what group is for. Group meetings are where and how we learn about building healthy connections. That's why group is so important. Group isn't magic (although magical things *do* happen there). If a spiritual awakening is the experience of gaining access to our insides, then group is often where that door opens. *Group is where readiness meets spirituality.*

Again, group itself isn't magic. If the people attending a specific group aren't growing, if there isn't any real self-revelation, risk, trust, and honesty occurring, then not much is going to happen in that group. Spirit seeks depth. Spirit is not made welcome in a place where there is no effort to go beyond the minimum.

Let's be honest here: *Addiction is a fatal disease.* Addiction is a unique form of insanity, as Step Two of the Twelve Steps clearly states (Week 10). Only the alcoholic/addict can know how true that is. There is no downward limit to the self-destructive thoughts, feelings, and physical unraveling of even an arrested addiction if ongoing recovery work is not done. There is nothing of goodness, family, peace, or sanity that addiction won't destroy if we don't do the hard work of recovery.

Recovery is not a game. It's not an "if I have time" or "if I feel like it" or "the least I can get away with" enterprise. Recovery is a deadly serious affair. As the wise AA saying goes, *all it takes is all there is.*

So where can you find safety? What is our defense against this insidious insanity? How is survival—let alone a life thriving in the Promises—to be won?

The answer is your group. The answer is to surround yourself with others who are committed to the same kind of "all the way in" recovery, people who clearly understand the dangerous situation their addiction has created.

The answer is to surround yourself with others who are living recovery principles and practicing their program for all they're worth.

The answer is to surround yourself with others who know what it means to hold the line against their particular kind of insanity and mental drunkenness.

The answer is to surround yourself with others who know how important it is to be there when a suffering brother or sister reaches out a hand for help.

The moment, the place, the event when such like-minded people come together to work on recovery principles, to remind each other of these principles, and to stand shoulder to shoulder against the common enemy *is* your group.

Group can get old. People can easily come to take their group for granted. The uniqueness of the group can come to be thought of as just another club or special interest event. Or worse. There are even Twelve Step groups where the program is totally betrayed.

But none of that eliminates what the group is meant to be—and *is* for those who seek out and demand for themselves the kind of active, honest, and real fellowship that their group can be.

Group is where a member says, "These are *my* people. These are the ones I march with. These are the people I cast my lot with—the folks I guard and defend, as I know they do me. It is with *these* people that I learn the lessons that addiction stole from me, lessons that take the form of spiritual awakenings that speak of trust and honesty and friendship and purpose. These are the people standing with me as I fend off the tragedy of spiritual bankruptcy—my brothers and sisters who walk with me into the life of the Promises."

Perfect? No. "Perfect" does not exist in this life. There are no perfect people and no perfect groups. But there are both people and groups that make all the difference in a recovering person's life. There are groups that are safe, loving, and honest. There are groups that will take the worst you have to tell them and in return give you your allotment of daily bread. There are groups within which you will find a new, better, deeper definition of *friend* than you have ever known before. Because these groups line up with the intention and purpose of the AA founders, they are the antidote to your hole in the soul.

• • •

Meet Ralph. Besides being an addict for forty years, he had done two tours in Vietnam. Of the thirteen men of his squad who came back from that long-ago war, eleven were going either to the stockade or to treatment. Ralph went to treatment. But he was a casualty of life long before he went to war. PTSD (post-traumatic stress disorder) was as much a part of him as his fingerprints many years before the bullets started flying.

I once had the honor of putting on a program with Ralph at a prison boot camp. He told the men that there was no hope of ongoing recovery if they didn't connect to their mates. He told them that he had to count on his fellow soldiers as much in recovery as he ever did walking point in the jungle. "The enemy is everywhere," he said solemnly.

Then he smiled at the inmates. He said he was certain that some of them knew darn well just what he was talking about. He explained that sometimes, at the oddest moments, maybe while walking down the street, he got a flashback that flipped him right back into the trauma. He said sweat would pour out of him, his heart would speed up, his head would pound, and his nerves would go into overdrive as if preparing to fend off a deadly attack.

At that point, Ralph told the inmates, he had to find a wall he could back up against so no one could get behind him. "When it hits," he said, "I can't tolerate people I don't know standing or walking behind me. What I do next," he continued, "is pull my personal soldiers around me. I call on my sponsor and group of men I walk with—the ones I trust. I let them surround me and give them my back. I hear them tell me that I'm okay. I'm safe. They say they will protect me and that it's okay to relax and let go. And eventually I do. It passes, and I can move on."

He told the inmates that maybe they wouldn't have to work as hard as he did to stay clean and sober. Maybe none of them knew what he was talking about when he told them about backing against a wall to protect himself. But maybe they did. He said we all have to find out what works for *us*. "And for me," he said, "I wouldn't walk around the block without my squad of soldiers going with me."

For Ralph, it was either use your group or say goodbye to recovery.

MAKE IT REAL

Some of you working through these weeks are already connected to strong, loving groups. You know what I'm talking about. Others, not so much or not at all. Some miss the importance of group because of a negative experience they had with one group or another along the way—and they failed to keep looking until they found a meeting they could call home. Others are wary of groups of any kind. Still others say they don't have time for a group. Whatever the reasons for skimping on meetings, for most people, if the group is not embraced and used, the pull back to active addiction proves too strong to resist. For the vast majority of people in recovery, their group is a *must*.

ACTION STEPS

Still not convinced that group fellowship is an essential part of your recovery? Sometimes it takes a while for the gift to be appreciated. As the old-timers so wisely advise, "Keep coming back!"

WRITE: (two or three paragraphs if you can, on the following topics. Give personal examples.)
1. Explain why "group is where readiness meets spirituality."
2. Describe two or three characteristics of a "good group" (honesty and friendliness, for example).

SHARE: (with your group or sponsor)
1. One or two ways in which your "group family" is the same as or different from your biological family.
2. Your need of the group's help in overcoming your tendency to hide or run away, for example.

CONSCIOUS CONTACT: Ask your Higher Power for the wisdom and strength to "keep coming back" no matter what.

• • •

• WEEK 35 •

Service Work

We have a very special guest presenter this week. His name is Fin, and he is a dear friend of mine who has been clean and sober for well over twenty years. He's one of those members of the Fellowship who never stops doing service work. In a healthy kind of way, service work is his life. He is a champion of *payback*. Fin has sponsored a good many people along the way, so I asked him to talk to us about the importance of service—at whatever point in your recovery. This is what he had to say:

My dearest friend Earnie,

I am writing this letter in response to your questions about the importance of service. All I really have to offer is my own experience, you know. Unfortunately, I don't know how to keep this brief, because service to others and to God has impacted every part of my life and my family's lives, too. My first real experience was at the group level. It started when my home group made me a greeter early on, a job I held for eleven years. Because I was still consumed with self, that was something I struggled with in the beginning. There were a lot of nights that I didn't want to shake anybody's hand or hug some little old lady. *But after a while, I became okay with it. Then I started to look forward to it. Then I came to rely upon it.*

How did that happen? I started to feel good about my interaction with others. The people I greeted got to know me and then began asking questions like "How are you doing?"

And gradually, I started to let these fine people in. That in turn started breaking me out of the isolation that so many of us feel when we first come in. Sometimes I would take my four-year-old son, Joe, with me. He'd stand across from me, and he would greet people as well. He'd extend his hand and say, "My name is Joe, and my dad is an alcoholic." Joe is going to be twenty-six in two weeks. Now he has seven months of sobriety—mostly because he knew where to go when he needed help. There's a lot of therapy in a handshake or a hug.

My next big experience with service came when I was four months sober. Lenny, a guy I went to treatment with, and I were asked to go back to that same treatment center to talk to some clients who were being discharged the next day. Our job was to let them know what to expect post-treatment—and to promote our Twelve Step program and aftercare. Lenny did the driving that night, and we made the seventy-minute drive through a blizzard. Did I mention that Lenny was blind in his left eye and had no depth perception in his right? The roads were horrible, and his driving didn't help. For me, it was a forced opportunity to improve my conscious contact with the God of my understanding, or as we call it up here, "take a quick Eleventh Step." The group we were speaking to was pretty receptive to our talk. There was a woman who was really scared to leave treatment because she had so many things to attend to on the outside—especially trying to get her kids back from the Children's Aid Society. She went into a meltdown and started screaming at everyone in the room. We all sat there quietly and let her have her venting session until she eventually calmed down. Afterward, she thanked us for keeping our cool, and we all hugged each other.

On the way home, Lenny and I realized how grateful we were. That episode also fueled my desire to help others. That whole evening took about five hours, and in all that time, I didn't think about my own crap even once. Service takes me out of myself. When I'm able to help another human being, I feel a real sense of satisfaction and self-worth. And when my self-esteem is low, I've found that the best way to combat that is to do something esteemable.

My service to others now extends outside AA. When I was two years sober, I won my first election as a union rep where I worked. I got to serve by representing the 5 percent that cause 95 percent of the problems. I used to be part of that 5 percent. I served two terms and then went on to another union position, that of an EAP/Substance Abuse Rep. Both jobs kept me very humble because every time I had contact with one of our membership, it reminded me of who I am (an alcoholic). I had a wonderful opportunity to help change lives in some small way. To be able to see a man or woman stand up and walk again. To see families reunited. To hear grateful spouses and their children say how glad they are to be a family again. I had a front row seat to all of that and more. I sponsor several men, and to watch them become whole again is a renewal of hope for *me*. Even though I have been sober for quite some time now, I still need to have hope renewed. I'm grateful that hope is a renewable resource.

A late mentor told me that service is like money in the bank—just keep putting it in and someday, when you need it, it will be there for you. That day came a little over five years ago when both our daughter and granddaughter died. The outpouring of love we received was unbelievable. The people around us carried my whole family for a long time afterward. A woman in the program did all of our house-work for ten days. She said it was her way of thanking me for getting her brother to the hospital when he had tried to commit suicide years earlier. People loaned us money for the down payment on the funeral. My sponsor sat up with me all night the day they died, and because he was up all night, he was able to take a call from the hospital saying that his dad had about a half-hour to live. (He would have missed that call if he'd been asleep.) So his service to another (me) enabled him to be there for his dad, who had fifty years of sobriety when he died. In God's world, nothing happens by mistake. The people who helped us through that tough period were all the same people I had the privilege of being involved with at some point.

After the funeral, the depression set in, and I didn't want to be around people. But our phone kept ringing for some sort of service, and even though I didn't want to go out, I did it anyway, and eventually I started to heal. Service helped to take me out of self. It really is true that if you want to keep it, you must give it away. Today I still keep busy with service work. I have spoken to medical students and nursing students several times in the last two years about AA and EAP. It's very humbling to have medical students ask me questions when every one of them is smarter than I will ever be. Even more important is when one of the students breaks down because of an addiction problem at home. *That is the reward for me, because we have reached one more person.* I've done three one-month workshops on the Twelve Steps, designed to help get newcomers into the recovery process. This workshop is called Back to Basics. It's how Bill and Dr. Bob took newcomers through the steps in the forties. Now we see a lot of those newcomers coming to our meetings—and a good many of them are on fire. Those people will now carry the message through their own service work.

Service has enabled me to meet some of the finest people in the world, and that certainly includes you, my friend. In June, I was invited to help out with a retreat weekend for codependents who attended the family program at the local treatment center. I presented the Fourth Step process to the six clients. I felt like a million dollars afterward because I knew I was doing something worthwhile. I cannot really explain the good feelings that service to others creates within me. It's like preventive medicine. You don't need a degree or have to work in the profession to do service. Sometimes service is as simple as shaking a man's hand and saying, "Welcome," or taking some poor guy out for a cup of coffee, or simply just listening to him. No big brain required. My service has also paid dividends in the help our son has received since he came into recovery.

If you're not giving it away, you really need to ask yourself why. The truth is you're missing out on the best our program has to offer. The man who Twelve-Stepped me says that *gratitude* is an action word. I believe the most important action is to make myself available to others, especially newcomers. I look forward to your next letter. I love you, my Brother.

Peace, Fin

A C T I O N   S T E P S

Old-timers often say that "more will be revealed." Understanding the exact nature of our character defects, for example, takes time and consistent willingness to make the effort. Service work is worth the effort. The reward? Freedom from the pull of the past.

WRITE: (two or three paragraphs if you can, on the following topics. Give personal examples.)

1. Do you understand why "*gratitude* is an action word"? Explain your thinking.
2. In addition to helping others, how does service work help *you*? Give two examples.

SHARE: (with your group or sponsor)

1. Tell when, where, and for whom you recently performed service work.
2. Tell about a time someone reached out to *you*. Explain what that meant to you.

CONSCIOUS CONTACT: Ask your Higher Power to raise your awareness of opportunities to help others.

PRACTICE: Stand by the door and greet newcomers to your meetings.

• • •

• **WEEK 36** •

Working the Steps

Weeks 21 through 25 were all about why the Steps work and how to practice them. If you can't quickly call to mind the lessons from those weeks, go back and review the work you did there.

The focus this week is on a specific part of working the Steps. We'll be studying the often-overlooked phrase in Step Five—that we "share the exact nature of our wrongs." Notice that it doesn't simply say "our wrongs" but the "*exact nature* of our wrongs."

Putting a cast on your leg when your arm is broken doesn't help much. Bringing ice skates to play a basketball game doesn't help much, either. Nor does reading the wrong chapter of an assignment before an exam. What helps is to *know the cause*. What helps is to zero in on the heart of what's causing the pain. What helps is the correct diagnosis of what is *really* wrong with us. That's what getting to the "exact nature of our wrongs" means.

According to the Big Book, (1) our problem is not alcohol or drugs. The problem at the heart of addiction is spiritual bankruptcy. (2) Spiritual bankruptcy reveals itself in our character defects. (3) Character defects are the insanity (Week 10) that blocks spiritual awakenings. (4) Spiritual awakenings (Step Twelve) are the *only* antidote to spiritual bankruptcy.

So the key here is to break through the logjam of character defects that stands between us and our recovery. This is the point of the Steps—to get to the "exact nature" of those character defects. The reason the founders put this phrase in the Steps is because we must understand the exact nature of our character defects before we can counter them. Once we do that, we open the way for spiritual awakenings—which allows us to fully embrace recovery and to finally get to some genuine self-compassion and self-love.

Missing the "exact nature of our wrongs" leads to some awfully sad situations when it comes to self-love.

Early on, all of us developed ways to meet the deepest need of the human heart—to find love and acceptance, the good stuff. Sometimes the methods we used were healthy and effective; for most addicts though, this wasn't the case. We did what we could to survive. We developed a coping technique, or "fastball" of sorts, in our quest for acceptance, intimacy, and spiritual connections. What did you learn that worked best for you? What were your most effective moves? What did you do to feel good enough or worthy enough or at least acceptable?

Whatever lessons you learned are still there, grinding away at the core of your existence—demanding, forbidding, acting out, and singing the same old song. *That* is what getting to the exact nature is all about. It's about discovering the exact nature of what is repeatedly slitting our recovery throats, so we can protect ourselves and move past it to find true intimacy and healthy connections.

So many of us never got beyond that so-called fastball, the specific behavior that didn't work then and doesn't work now. We never learned healthy ways to meet the needs of our hearts, so we keep doing the same old things we hated ourselves for doing in the past. We don't understand why we act this way, and this failure to understand that "why" (the exact nature) pretty much dooms us to go on doing whatever "it" may be.

Some of us learned the only way we were wanted or allowed to hang around was by letting others use our bodies for their selfish pleasure. We hated it then, and we hate it now. But that's the way we learned to find love and acceptance. Now that we're in recovery, we feel scared when the genuine intimacy of the Fellowship comes walking down the road toward us. We don't trust. Being loved for who we are is *new* and doesn't feel right. We may react by running back to the hiding place we know (the exact nature). We use our bodies as a calling card, do what we most hate, and end up hurt and disappointed when someone responds to that calling card.

The Steps tell us to get to the exact nature of our vulnerability so we can push on through it and come out on the other side.

Some of us learned that the only way we were wanted or allowed to hang around was by being tough. We learned to take a punch—often a physical punch, but always an emotional one. We practiced until we couldn't be hit hard enough to put us down or keep us down. We learned to stand knee-deep in our own blood, daring whatever power was beating the hell out of us to give us its best shot. When it was done, we'd still be standing. We learned to endure. So now, when the real intimacy of the program comes walking down the road toward us, we run back to the hiding place we knew (the exact nature). Old-timers and sponsors tell us that recovery is to be joyful. They tell us that life can be more than an endurance contest—that it's okay to relax, to drop our guard, to allow ourselves to be loved in the Fellowship. But it is so *new* we don't trust it. Again and again, we push away Fellowship to prove (to whom?) that "I can make it alone. I don't need anyone to be there for me."

The Steps tell us to get to the exact nature of our vulnerability so we can push on through and get to the other side.

Some of us learned the only way we were wanted or allowed to hang around was to be a doormat. We learned that our role in life was to be everyone else's answer. *Their* wants and needs (no matter how selfish) were our number one responsibility. We—our essence, our very spirits—were pushed aside during an insane rush to make life wonderful for someone or everyone else. We got stepped on, stomped on, betrayed, and left out to dry countless times, but we never said *no*. We became helplessly, hopelessly dependent on others for approval and validation. It didn't work then, and it doesn't work now. So now, when real program intimacy approaches, we run back to the hiding place we knew (the exact nature). We're more than willing to sell our integrity and self-respect for a pseudo sense of belonging to someone. We get conned again and hate ourselves for falling for that same old line.

The Steps tell us to get to the exact nature of our vulnerabilities so we can push on through and get to the other side.

These are just some of the ways that addicts have learned to get the good stuff. Others used different "fastballs," such as

- feeling rather than thinking
- thinking rather then feeling
- screaming and threatening
- never saying no
- putting on a show
- always being useful to others
- shutting up, staying out of the way
- never objecting or complaining
- insisting on being first
- whining and crying
- paying for everything
- insisting that we are always right

"The exact nature of our wrongs" is our personal poison. What was *your* poison? How did you use that poison, or fastball, to deflect genuine connections and fellowship? How did you learn to get the good stuff? Did it work then? Does it work now? Back in the day, whatever you learned may well have saved your life. But what about *now*? How is it working for you now?

MAKE IT REAL

Yes, this is hard ground to plow. Quite naturally, none of us wants to get too close to what really hurts inside of us. But a commitment to recovery must include a commitment to what it takes to *stay* in recovery. And clearly the founders of AA thought it vitally important to get to the exact nature of our wrongs, or they wouldn't have put it in the Steps. *This work is worth the effort.*

ACTION STEPS

After years of polishing up our story, it isn't easy to get honest about who we really are and how we've really operated. It may take quite a while to stop dancing around and finally come to grips with the truth. Be patient; expect frustration. The prize awaits you! Just keep on keeping on.

WRITE: (two or three paragraphs if you can, on the following topics. Give personal examples.)
1. Explain what the phrase "the exact nature of our wrongs" means to you.
2. Give three examples of how "the exact nature of your wrongs" has blocked your progress in recovery.

SHARE: (with your group or sponsor)
1. Tell your group what your "fastball" has been. Give an example of how you used it.
2. Explain the relationship between using your fastball and the growth of self-respect.

CONSCIOUS CONTACT: Thank your Higher Power for the opportunity to learn better responses to life's challenges.

• • •

• WEEK 37 •

Study the Big Book

This week we have another guest presenter. Still in new recovery, Rick was just about a year sober at this writing. He volunteered to talk to you about the value of the Big Book and how his sponsor took him through the wisdom available there for all of us. Take a lesson from his recovery story:

I was told that the Big Book is the textbook of the Fellowship of Alcoholics Anonymous, and within that text is a program of action that will enable you to find a Power greater than yourself to solve your problem.

That's what they told me anyway. So I tried reading the first 164 pages (while resenting those Big Book geeks who kept quoting page numbers and sayings) and found it to be . . . quite stuffy! That was pretty typical of me—to think and then figure it out all by myself. (But look where that had gotten me!)

I'd been attending AA meetings for two months and was enjoying my new friends. At some meetings, we talked about the Twelve Steps and what they meant to everyone. Sometimes there was talk of sponsors and the different ways that a good sponsor could help you. In the back (maybe even the front) of my mind, I figured I'd get to that "sponsor stuff" soon enough.

Then my Higher Power stepped in. Through a series of unlikely events, I happened to meet a guy who said to me, "I need to be working the Steps all the time. Would you be willing to read the Big Book with me?" He was pretty clear that it would be mostly for *him,* because that was what he did to stay sober.

So one day we sat side by side on a bench and opened our Big Books. Then Paul began to read to me. We started with the blank page at the beginning, moved into the foreword, The Doctor's Opinion, Bill's Story, and so on. As he read, mixing in a lot of his personal experiences, I found myself taking a lot of notes in the margins of my book. I began to understand that this material really was relevant to *us* and not just a seventy-year-old volume of stuff that used to be effective. And it was clear that, like so many others in AA, Paul believed that what worked for the original one hundred drunks would still work for us.

One day Paul said to me, "I've gone through this process with dozens and dozens of guys. Ya know what my track record is?" I thought about it for a second, but before I could answer he said, "100 percent!" "This guy is *good,*" I thought. "I'm pretty fortunate." Paul was grinning because he knew I *didn't* get it. When he added, "Because I'm still sober," it finally hit me. He really *was* doing it for himself—with the sincere hope that I would completely give myself over to the program and maintain my sobriety just as he had.

As we kept reading, I learned that I have a mental obsession I couldn't possibly get over without help—help from the often-mentioned and frequently misunderstood Higher Power. That mental obsession is what led to my first drink, which caused the physical craving to kick in—and we all know the rest. On page 30, Paul and I began Step One. We talked about it extensively, which gave me a new understanding of powerlessness. Step Two's instructions were on page 47, Step Three's on page 63. I had read this darn book three separate times, and I *still* didn't have a clue how detailed, specific, and *simple* it was. But Paul knew.

As Paul continued to share his experience and strength, I actually began to hope that this process really could change things in my life. I had heard many people talk about how they were stuck on their Fourth Step and were *not* looking forward to moving on to their Fifth Step. Paul walked me through the instruction for Step Four over a three-week period (one for resentments, one for fears, and one for sexual conduct). There was no pausing or resting. We approached the material with sincerity and our combined resolve. The following week we did Step Five. Then after six-and-a-half hours of bone-crushing honesty, tears, and laughter (how many times can the same character defect come up over a thirty-year period before you just have to laugh?), we finished.

Then something unexpected happened. I went home and read the Fifth Step promises on page 75—and *they were precisely what I was feeling!* I began to realize that this "spiritual awakening" thing was not all that mystical. *It was already happening in me.* A great wave of peace came over me, and I felt an outpouring of extreme gratitude. I called a few of my new friends and shared the feeling with them. To this day, they occasionally recall this sharing and tell *me* how grateful *they* are that I passed my gratitude along to them.

So—is this how you form friendship bonds?

Paul and I went on to do Step Six and Step Seven, moved on to Step Eight, and laid the groundwork for Step Nine. He's still just a phone call away if I run into difficulty making my amends. I won't say it hasn't been difficult, but I feel calmly driven to finish the job.

Step Ten has been an absolute joy to make part of my daily life. These days, I think more about the way I treat people—and if something just sticks in my head, chances are I've wronged someone. It really isn't that hard to say, "Oops, I regret what I've done!" and then go on with a new perspective on how to behave next time.

Conscious contact with God. Hmmm . . .

Step Eleven came fast and with intensity. I felt very close to the God of my understanding—but it was like he took the gloves off and just let his love pour over me. Hard to explain, easy to receive.

For me, the focus of Step Twelve had always been the spiritual awakening. Now I learned from Paul what is meant by the phrase "We tried to carry this message to alcoholics and practice these principles in all our affairs." Actually, Paul didn't need to say a word; he'd been demonstrating it to me for more than four months. We reached the point we'd been building toward for weeks—and gratitude just overwhelmed me as I realized I would someday have the chance to sit with a fellow drunk and "read the book" with him.

Can you picture us two men, one fifty-three and one sixty-eight, sitting on a bench in the sunshine on a Sunday afternoon? Both of us were crying quietly in deep gratitude for this shared experience and peacefully aware of the nearness of our Creator.

Out of all the lessons I most treasure from this experience, two stand out: The first is the *insanity of thinking I could do this alone.* I understand why I approached it that way at first. That's what I always used to do—think it out but stay isolated. Well, this program works best when you take action and leave what little thinking is required to the other guy (your sponsor!). The second lesson is about *God, Higher Power, or whatever phrase you choose.* I used to think that when Bill and the first hundred wrote the Big Book, they watered down the God aspect because they wanted to make it easier on those of us who would be resistant. Now I truly understand why the "God of your understanding" is how they worded it. I believe it's because your relationship with your Higher Power becomes so personal, so familiar, so loving, so unique, so essential, and so intimate that the first hundred didn't want to even come close to implying that *they* would understand exactly who *your* God was—only that it would be a wonderful and everlasting relationship.

In the book *Pass It On: The Story of Bill Wilson and How the A.A. Message Reached the World,* a man told the following story about meeting Bill W.: "I was a couple of months sober and was so excited, so thrilled to meet the co-founder that I gushed all over him with what my sobriety meant to me and my undying gratitude for his starting AA. When I finally ran down, Bill calmly took my hand in his and simply said, 'Pass it on.'"

In gratitude to my sponsor, Paul, I'll express it continually in all my efforts to "pass it on."

ACTION STEPS

If you haven't immersed yourself in the Big Book, you are missing a most powerful aid to joyful, ongoing recovery. Rick did us a great favor by sharing his experience, strength, and hope. Let us all take it to heart.

WRITE: (two or three paragraphs if you can, on the following topics. Give personal examples.)
1. Two or three reasons why it's a good idea to read the Big Book with someone else.
2. Explain what the Big Book says about "powerlessness" in its discussion of the First Step.

SHARE: (with your group or sponsor)
1. Read aloud your favorite quote from the Big Book and explain what it means to you.
2. Ask experienced members of your group to talk about the value of the Big Book in their ongoing recovery.

CONSCIOUS CONTACT: Ask your Higher Power to open your mind and heart to the wisdom of the Big Book.

REACH OUT: Give a Big Book to a new member who doesn't have one.

• • •

• WEEK 38 •

Practice Forgiveness

Hold on to your hats! I recently heard this wild story at an open meeting.

I don't remember the storyteller's name. Let's call her Mary. She now has seventeen years in the Fellowship. Early on in her recovery, she said, her husband of nineteen years (in and out of the Fellowship) left her to go off with the "office skank." Mary, of course, was outraged, humiliated, infuriated, and every other kind of "-iated" she could think of. To Mary, her husband's departure with a young woman put him squarely in the "UB club"—universal bastard. Mary said she was on the verge of throwing away her sobriety "just to teach him a lesson." She wondered if the program had a special escape clause that covered murdering someone who so richly deserved it. (If it didn't, she sure thought it should!)

Mary told us that her sponsor let her vent, gripe, complain, and sit on her pity pot for a few weeks. But then, Mary went on, "We had a 'come to Jesus' meeting."

Her sponsor told Mary that she'd given her soon-to-be ex-husband enough of her time and energy. "Now," she said, "it's time to put things in their right place and move on."

"What are you saying?" Mary gasped. "Can't you tell I have a broken heart? Don't you even *care?*"

"Yes, I care," her sponsor said. "I care too much to watch you go on acting like such a ninny. It's time to move on."

"How?" Mary asked.

"Simple," said her sponsor. "You forgive him. You forgive him because you can't afford not to. Your resentment is costing you too much."

Mary was born for the stage. A very stylish woman in her fifties, she had beautiful red hair and big blue eyes. It was a treat to watch her tell her story. Her face was amazingly animated. Her body language and hand gestures were those of an Academy Award-winning actress. In fact, Mary didn't just *tell* her story—she communicated it so well she *was* her story. No words of mine could describe the way she communicated the fit she had upon hearing this advice. Imagine the audacity of someone, even her sponsor, suggesting that she needed to forgive her UB husband!

"Forgive?" she shouted. "How could anyone be asked to forgive someone who did something so evil?" Her red hair seemed to turn to flame as she tossed her head.

Many in the audience appeared to relate to what she was talking about. I guess a lot of us had our own UBs on our mental "get even list." Surely there are reasonable limits to the forgiveness directive in the program!

Mary went on to tell how her sponsor kept working her through this spiritual logjam she was up against. She told Mary to think about what part of the breakup might have been her fault. What had she contributed to the marriage failing?

Mary's sponsor wasn't asking her to take the blame for what had happened. She was asking Mary to honestly admit and accept that some part of the pain of her husband leaving her might have had something to do with all the years she was in active addiction during their marriage. Mary said that when she finally got totally honest, her sponsor helped her see that she hadn't been totally faithful in her marriage, either—especially not in her using days.

Her sponsor told her to get realistic about the stones she was throwing. If she was going to throw them at someone else, she had to get ready to take some incoming rocks herself.

Mary went on to tell us that for a while she, her ex, and his new girlfriend, Joan, all went to the same meetings. The new girlfriend got pregnant, and soon Mary's ex left Joan, too, for another woman he thought would take better care of him. But rather than saying, "Good! You got what was coming to you!" Mary said that she and

Joan actually started talking—and before long became friends. Two years later a real tragedy happened—Joan's baby died.

Calm as a judge now, Mary told us about the baby's funeral. Joan apparently didn't have any family, or at least no one she was close to. The father was nowhere to be found. Joan asked Mary to walk with her behind the tiny casket as it was wheeled into church. "We sat together holding hands," Mary said, "and both of us wept." Finally, Mary said that she was honored and grateful beyond all words to have been allowed to play a part in her new friend's life.

Mary's message was that there is no such thing as "a wrong too bad to forgive." Not because people aren't capable of gutting each other, but because the cost of refusing to forgive is too high. "Who would have lost," Mary asked us, "if I had climbed up on my high horse and refused to forgive a wrong that I had a part in? Besides," she said, "getting out of my life turned out to be the greatest thing my husband could have done for me."

The point is that forgiveness has nothing to do with "them." It's not about how deserving they are of forgiveness, or about whether they've admitted what they've done to you. *Forgiveness is a gift you give yourself.* It's the decision you make to be done with paying the price of resentment and to free your spirit of the burden created by *not* forgiving. *The fact is that what you will not let go of will not let go of you.* Forgiveness is all about letting go.

COLLATERAL BLESSINGS

Collateral damage is a term used by people in the violence business. Suppose the goal is to exert "extreme prejudice" against an enemy by setting off a bomb or lobbing an artillery shell at them. If the intended target is "erased" and ten innocent people are also killed, well, that's just "collateral damage." Those who measure the acceptability of such damage usually regard the loss as regrettable but acceptable if the goal is reached. (But don't you have to wonder if the "loss" would be acceptable if *they* were the ones standing in the wrong place at the wrong time?)

Collateral blessings, on the other hand, are the ripples of goodness, healing, and spirituality that radiate from an act of forgiveness.

These blessings may well be unintended—you had no idea that anyone was watching, but they were. And they were touched and blessed and sometimes changed by what they saw in your act of forgiveness.

Here's another thought: The spiritual blessing of forgiveness you offered another may well have affected the way the receiver interacted with dozens of people you will never know or hear about. Perhaps they, in their turn, will offer the same blessing to those they meet—and on and on. The spiritual root of all this goodness, were it known and somehow traced back, would be your act of forgiveness. *It started with you.* Just as yours may have started with someone else who has no idea how he or she blessed you.

Without forgiveness, the world is a wasteland full of weeping and gnashing of teeth. Forgiveness, first of self and then extending to all the others who cross your path, is the key that sets a person free.[3]

ACTION STEPS

Forgiveness is most necessary when you feel personally wronged. That's why forgiving so often demands courage and breadth of spirit. It's so easy to hang on to "justified resentments"—and fail to see that the only person being hurt is the one who refuses to let go of the pain. If you are hanging on to any resentments, even "justified resentments," *please do this work.*

WRITE: (two or three paragraphs if you can, on the following topics. Give personal examples.)

1. Make a list of all those you have not forgiven, starting with yourself.
2. Describe the price you are paying for withholding forgiveness. How is the resentment adding to the isolation and "hole in your soul" at the center of your addiction (Week 8)?

---

[3] For a fuller treatment of anger and forgiveness, see *From Anger to Forgiveness,* a Hazelden book by Earnie Larsen with Carol Larsen Hegarty.

SHARE: (with your group or sponsor)
1. Ask your sponsor or group to provide the support and strength you need to take the critical step of actualizing forgiveness.
2. Talk about any particular difficulty you're having in forgiving yourself.

CONSCIOUS CONTACT: Thank your Higher Power for the chance to finally make peace with the past.

PRACTICE: Humbly ask forgiveness from someone *you* have hurt.

• • •

• WEEK 39 •

Demanding Joy

This week we have another guest presenter. Her name is Kendra S., and when you read her story, you'll know why I asked her to say a few words about having fun in recovery. By way of introduction, Kendra rides a Harley. She's part of a group of men and women in the Fellowship who do a lot of bike rides, mostly on weekends. It's quite a sight when they all show up—at church, for example. Lots of noise, flags, joking, laughing—and some of the best program you'll ever find. Here is what Kendra has to share with us:

I've finally accepted that balance is something that I'll just *always* have to strive for. But over the years, I still maintain my initial resolve—from that very first time I walked through these doors of AA, court-ordered and bitter about having to walk down this path of sober living.

I was so fearful that it was going to mean the end of ever having a good time and enjoying life again! Being in my mid-twenties, I was just too darn young to quit having fun. So I made a promise to myself right then and there that if I couldn't have fun in sobriety, I could always go back out there and "do more research," as they say. Maybe this wasn't the best outlook to have—but it has worked for me all these years.

Since then, I've discovered what it truly means to have fun. I love the beginning of chapter 11 (A Vision for You) in our Big Book, the line that says, "drinking means conviviality, companionship, and colorful imagination." Now *that* describes what

I've found in our Fellowship of AA—the priceless connection I can make with others. Believe me, there's nothing better than deep gut laughter that brings tears to your eyes—something I've been so richly blessed with in sobriety. I've had a blast in AA, whether it's going to coffee after a meeting with some friends, going out dancing for the first time sober, or challenging myself to pursue dreams that I'd previously not even allowed myself to consider, such as getting my motorcycle endorsement and going on lots of bike trips. I just never could have imagined doing such fun things sober!

Today, it's so much fun to get together with other sober pals and enjoy dancing, motorcycling, concerts, barbecues, bonfires, races, camping, bowling, house parties, game nights, comedy shows—all kinds of options out there! Life is for the living, and I want to experience as much as possible. What a treasure it is to have this gift of life and my second chance to really *live.*

In my twenty-plus years of sobriety, I've sponsored many, *many* new gals in the program. At first—like me when I started—there's often a period of doubts and questions as the new person struggles with figuring out what this new life is all about. So right at the beginning, I make sure my new sponsees understand that the AA way of life is *anything* but a sad, gloomy endurance contest. I tell them, "If you're going to be miserable, you might as well go back and drink." I so believe that is true. Lucky for me—and all of us—that is not the case.

So early on I get with my new sponsee and I ask, "Okay, what's fun for *you*? What makes you laugh? What can you do to have a good time and not feel rotten about it the day after?" What we do is make a "fun list." No doubt a lot of rigid old-timers wouldn't think much of a sponsor stressing something like a fun list. But what works for me—what *has to be* there for me in my program—is a way to hoot and holler and kick up my heels. I think life is meant to be enjoyed, whether a person is alcoholic or not. The only thing is that we have to find a way to do the hooting and hollering in a healthy, sober way. And I've found that "sober" is the best way ever to have fun and enjoy life.

If anyone reading this is sober but miserable, come over here. I'll help you make a fun list and get you on your way!

ACTION STEPS

For some people, like Kendra, having fun is *very* important. It's what they're all about. Others find giving themselves permission to have fun is a steep hill to climb. If *you're* good at fun, you probably read this week's topic and said, "Amen! You go, girl." For those who don't shine in this department, the work suggested this week may be more difficult to do, but it's important. If you're miserable, you're probably hanging around with the wrong people and not being creative enough. It's important to take fun seriously in recovery.

WRITE: (two or three paragraphs if you can, on the following topics. Give personal examples.)
  1. On a scale of 1 to 10 (1 being low and 10 high), how much enjoyment are you finding in your recovery?
  2. If you haven't made a fun list, begin by naming three things you find enjoyable or entertaining.

SHARE: (with your group or sponsor)
  1. Ask members of your group to share what *they* do to have fun.
  2. Tell about an activity you think would be a lot of fun—perhaps something you used to do and would like to do again. (Hint: go to a ballgame or play cards, for example.)

CONSCIOUS CONTACT: Ask your Higher Power to lead you to jolly (but safe) companions.

REACH OUT: Ask friends in the program to join you for an enjoyable activity. Make a plan. Set a date. Take the initiative!

• • •

SECTION 9

Regarding Relationships

• **WEEK 40** •

Where the Power Is

Over the next five weeks, we're going to look at several key issues regarding relationships. Relationships—the agony and the ecstasy. Relationships—flashpoint of countless relapses but also the vital connections that give wings to our recovery. Staying connected means starting and staying in healthy relationships.

I've taught this material often enough to have heard a lot of criticism from some people in recovery. They're folks who fancy themselves independent, tough, and more than able to "stand on their own two feet." They insist they can do without this kind of "touchy-feely stuff."

Such people consider themselves strong willed and strong minded, I guess. I respectfully suggest that what they are is perhaps not so much strong as afraid. Surrendering to the power and care of the Fellowship is frightening. It's downright terrifying to a person who's never allowed anyone to get close before. The "exact nature" of our character defects—which blocks spirituality and therefore relationships—goes all the way to the hole in the soul. It is the "exact nature of our wrongs" (Week 36) that deepens the hole in the soul and fuels our spiritual bankruptcy.

Recovery is all about dealing with the hole in the soul. It's all about recognizing and grabbing the rope of relationship the program throws out to help us climb up and out of isolation. In fact, the hole in the soul and its first-born child, isolation, are *specifically* created when we will not and cannot let anyone else—including the God of our understanding—get close to us.

Our hearts never stop yearning for connection. We're human; that's how we're made. The power of relationship (staying connected to your Higher Power, self, and others) is the only thing in this world strong enough to deal with the inner emptiness (the hole in the soul) every active addict experiences. *Recovery can only rise up on the wings of relationship.* That's why getting a handle on relationships is critical—not only for sobriety but also for ongoing recovery. The life of the Promises can only be ours if we take the spiritual medicine of relationship.

Let's begin by looking at the anatomy of relationships. What makes them work? What makes them fail, and what can we do about it? Is there any kind of "relationship insurance" we can take out? (Actually, there is. It's called working a solid, focused, intelligent, consistent program. It's called staying on your square no matter what's going on around you.)

As I mentioned earlier, people come up with all kinds of reasons for not getting to the heart of recovery work. And the heart of this work always includes opening up and reaching out to those all-important honest, humble connections with your Higher Power, self, and others. It's always about relationships. It's always spiritual. And at the heart of this spirituality is *grace.* Grace is the power to make positive (often seemingly impossible) changes in your life, as my friend Mick was able to do.

I know that for some people Mick's story may seem extreme. I thought long and hard about using a more familiar example to illustrate the importance and power of relationships. After all, *every successful recovery story reflects the power of relationships—with your Higher Power, self, and others.* Why? Because our problem is spiritual bankruptcy, with isolation as its main symptom (weeks 8 through 10). But Mick's story demanded to be told. So here it is.

Neither Mick nor I were yet thirty years old when we met at an Alano Club. Mick had just gotten out of prison for the third time. He was as handsome and hard as they come. Mick was a drug dealer and an armed hold-up man. "I only held up blind pigs, dope dens, and whorehouses," he said. "I knew they weren't going to call the cops." He was a hit man and street thug. He told me that he committed his first crime at age five. He'd been a lookout for a gang of older kids in his neighborhood as they stole things off a train on a siderail. Crime, dealing, and using were all Mick knew. When he first went to prison at eighteen, he said it was no big deal. Why? "Because half my neighborhood was already there. It was like old home week."

But Mick met something tougher than weapons and needles in prison. He met Frank. Frank was a lifer. He was never going to get out of prison. Frank was kind of a legend at this maximum security facility. No one messed with Frank. For some reason, Frank took a liking to Mick. He reached out to him in the only way anyone could have reached the young man. "You think you're tough," Frank said. "*You* aren't tough. Tough isn't about shanking people and making them afraid of you. Tough is about having control of yourself. You aren't in control of yourself. That spud juice you're always high on is in control of you!" (Mick's group worked in the kitchen. One of the things they fermented and turned into high-test alcohol was potatoes. That's where the term "spud juice" came from.)

To make a long story short, Frank took Mick under his wing. Frank had found AA while in prison and, even though he was never going to see the street again, he prized his sobriety. *Prison walls are no barrier to grace.*

In time, Mick also became a member of the Fellowship, with Frank as his sponsor. Our Alano Club was the first place Mick went after being released. This man who had once been a career criminal, a person everyone had given up on, now channeled all of his fervor and passion into his recovery. To say the *least,* Mick was a Twelve Step warrior.

Mick loved fancy clothes. For Christmas one year he bought a blue suede jacket. He loved that coat. Late one night, he called and told me to get down to the flophouse where we took men who'd passed out in the cold so they wouldn't freeze to death. He said one old man he'd picked up was vomiting blood, and he was afraid he would die. Mick insisted we get him to a hospital ASAP. When I got down there, Mick was standing under a single, naked lightbulb that was hanging over the front door of the flophouse. I noticed that the old man's blood, and whatever else he had had in his stomach, was all over Mick's prized jacket. He didn't mention his ruined jacket; he just said, "We got to save this old guy. He belongs to someone."

The power of relationship works miracles. Frank reached out to

Mick, and Mick reached out to this old man and many, many others. Every recovery story is a story of the power of relationships.

ACTION STEPS

This work is *so* worth the effort! Take the time. Make the effort. Do the work. See yourself and your recovery reflected back to you in the mirror of relationship.

WRITE: (two or three paragraphs if you can, on the following topics. Give personal examples.)
1. List the three most important relationships you've made so far in your recovery.
2. What have you learned and how have you changed as a result of these relationships?

SHARE: (with your group or sponsor)
1. Details about the two or three most significant relationships you've had in your life.
2. Your plan for repairing an important relationship that you've neglected or abused.

CONSCIOUS CONTACT: Ask your Higher Power for the willingness and the courage to be truly open to healthy relationships.

REACH OUT: Ask one or two group members to regularly meet with you so you can get to know each other better.

• • •

• WEEK 41 •

Relationships Require Skills

Loving and the ability to make relationships work are two different things entirely. "Wanting to" is not the same as "being able to."

If you review the weeks in this book dealing with the Steps (weeks 21 through 25), you'll find a map to relationship building. Working a good, focused, intelligent program is the world's best relationship counseling course.

Character defects block spirituality. Spirituality is a "between" thing—meaning spirituality "exists between two poles, creating at both ends." Spirituality exists *between* people and their Higher Power, between self and others. Spirituality is the awareness, the tenderness, the strength, and the courage that gives meaning to life. Like between Betty and the little boy at church.

Betty has been in recovery for two years now. Her mother was a drug addict before, during, and after her birth, and she never knew her father. Betty was a stripper "and other things I'd just as soon not talk about" by her fifteenth birthday. That was the same year she had her first child. The hole in her soul grew bigger than all the oceans combined.

But the miracle of a First Step came for her. Betty got up, found recovery, and started walking down a different path. Why her and not all the other women she "worked the pole with"? Who knows? Why all of you and not the army of alcoholics/addicts who will never get a second chance? Who knows?

Betty is doing better now. Her spirituality is saving her. But that doesn't mean the hole in her soul doesn't show through. I noticed her a few weeks ago at the church we both attend, a church that is a draw for a lot of recovering people. On that day, Betty was lovingly stroking the head of a little boy who had come over to sit next to her. For some reason, she's a magnet for children. Perhaps the little girl inside her connects with children. It may well be that the powerful love, gentleness, and protection she gives them surges out from that place in her that never knew such gifts. The children sense that, I guess.

Picture Betty stroking the little boy's head. Amazing grace flowing both ways—from Betty to the little boy and from the little boy back to Betty. This lovely picture clearly shows how the spirit exists in the "between," creating at both ends.

It's been famously said that "there's no spiritual side to recovery. It's *all* spiritual." So too, there is no spiritual side to a relationship. When relationships are working, it's all spiritual. The reverse is true when relationships fail. It's because the depth of spirituality is not sufficient to overcome the obstacles present in every relationship.

So we're back to the question "What blocks spirituality?" Not surprisingly, it's the same obstacles that block relationships. In program language, those obstacles are called "character defects," "insanity," our "wrongs," or "flawed thinking." In the extreme, it's called "spiritual bankruptcy." The solution to spiritual bankruptcy is also the solution to making relationships work. It requires practicing a new way of life built on recovery values rather than the values that lead to relapse.

What types of values?

The spirituality of relationship demands these values and skills:

- trust
- honesty
- humility
- commitment
- compromise

Are you willing to address the obstacles that block your ability to bring these values and skills to your relationship? Getting clean and sober does not automatically create these skills. Getting clean and sober only puts you in position to begin developing these skills by "having had a spiritual awakening as the result of working these

Steps." Getting to the "exact nature of our wrongs"—which Step Five tells us *is* working the Steps—is key in making relationships work, just as a getting correct diagnosis is key in treating any other life-threatening disease.

I call this list of five traits "skills" because any and all of them can be learned. It's never too late. Certainly, people can choose at any point not to go further or deeper than the ground they've won in their recovery walk. Such a decision is perfectly understandable. All of us have a right to say "enough" in our journey of recovery. But wherever you stop, there your spiritual journey also stops. That is, unless and until your life again begins to hurt too much because of "unfinished business." Spirit always seeks depth. You may well say, "Oh no, not this again? I thought I dealt with that a long time ago." And maybe you did, but now a deeper level is calling out for the healing touch of recovery principles.

Under every angry, violent relationship failure is a spiritual wound, character defect, blockage of the spirit, or widening of the hole in the soul. By whatever name, it's an energy vampire that will return again and again until you get to the cause, as the Steps direct, and tackle the *real* problem.

MAKE IT REAL

This is hard, scary work. Yes it is. Most of us would rather do most anything than take a hard look at the past *and* take responsibility for whatever part we've played in the health or weakness of our relationships. If there's a "softer, easier way" that works, fine. Let's all jump on that bus. But experience tells us that there *is* no softer, easier way. There is only *through*. So doing this work is essential to a future of undertaking, forming, and enjoying healthy relationships.

ACTION STEPS

A wise person once said, "There is no such thing as a happy marriage. There is only such a thing as two happy people who happen to be married." In other words, it takes personal okayness to bring okayness to a relationship. The bottom line? Qualify yourself by working the Steps!

WRITE: (two or three paragraphs if you can, on the following topics. Give personal examples.)

1. Which one or two of the five "relationship skills" listed on page 206 do you most need to work on?
2. What seems to block your ability to _____? (Choose one of the following: *trust, be honest, be humble, commit, compromise.*)

SHARE: (with your group or sponsor)

1. A specific example of your own contribution to a damaged or failed relationship.
2. Your understanding of this truism: "The obstacles that block spirituality are the same obstacles that block relationships."

CONSCIOUS CONTACT: Thank your Higher Power for the chance to become a better partner in relationship.

REACH OUT: If appropriate, ask your partner's forgiveness for your part in damaging your relationship.

• • •

• WEEK 42 •

The Elements of a Relationship

It's often said that people can't love others more than they love themselves. That's nonsense. It misses the point.

Countless addicts love others more than they love themselves. In fact many, many alcoholics/addicts use their chemicals to medicate the pain of just that fact. They continue to drink or use drugs precisely because they *do* love others and *know* the hurt and misery they are causing their loved ones—and they can't face the pain.

That said, addiction is a primary disease. Alcoholics/addicts don't need a reason to use. They use simply because they are alcoholics/addicts.

As I've said again and again throughout this book, recovery is about a whole lot more than not using chemicals. Recovery is about finding a way to heal the "hole in the soul." To heal it, you must first find it. You must find and name the attack dogs (your character defects) that stand guard around the expanding spiritual hole at your core—and every other addict's core as well. You must find the "exact nature" of what you use to deflect fellowship, love, belonging, and connectedness (Week 36). That means, "What stands in the way of your initiating and continuing in successful, positive, loving relationships?"

It's not true that you can't love others if you don't love yourself. The truth is, what you can't do is carry on a healthy relationship without first loving yourself. Loving and making relationships work are two totally different things.

Making relationships work requires *skills*, not just goodwill. You may love to eat, but that doesn't mean you can cook. You may love music, but that doesn't mean you know how to play an instrument. You may love basketball, but that doesn't mean you can play the sport.

That's why *self* is the first and only place to start thinking about—let alone doing something about—relationships. It starts with *you*. It starts with your commitment to *do something* about the well-trained guard dogs you've stationed all around your heart to fend off intimacy. To one degree or another, you've been doing this all your life. By now, those guard dogs have had a lot of practice, and they know what they're doing!

So what is your "relationship IQ"? How well do you understand why you pick the people you do and behave as you do in relationships? Let me once again list some examples of the "exact nature" of our guard dogs from Week 36. Why? Because if you can relate to any of these examples—if you can stand up and shout, "Yup, that's me!"—those dogs are still on the prowl around your heart, big as bulls and just as strong. *Relationships simply cannot grow in such an environment.*

Look at the list again:

- feeling rather than thinking
- thinking rather then feeling
- screaming and threatening
- never saying no
- putting on a show
- always being useful to others
- shutting up, staying out of the way
- always being tough
- denying our own needs
- never objecting or complaining
- insisting on being first
- whining and crying
- paying for everything
- insisting that we are always right
- allowing others to use our bodies
- being a doormat/always putting others first

Choose the one you most identify with. Hold it up. Look at it. Notice how it feels. Now use it like an old home movie, taking your time to review your history of relationships through that trait. At every opportunity for fellowship, "turning your life over to the care of the God of your understanding," trusting someone else, allowing yourself to be vulnerable—what did your own personal attack dog do to that possible relationship?

See if you relate to this example:

Alice and Jim are both in recovery. Each of them has about five years in the program. After two years clean and sober, they figured they were "good to go" for a relationship. In this case, the relationship went all the way to marriage.

After three years, their marriage is in trouble. Neither one of them is getting what they need or want from the marriage. In the two years of clean time that they each had before they got together, neither of them had identified the "exact nature" of their wrongs. So they carried that baggage with them into their marriage.

When that was explained to them, and they finally started looking at their lives through the lens of the "exact nature," blood-red flags sprang up. In the light of what they were now recognizing, they both said, "Well, damn! No wonder we're having all these problems."

Alice related big time to the example of the "tough guy." For all kinds of understandable reasons—once you knew where to look—this tough girl stood on her own two feet, didn't really need anyone else, and could take anything life could dish out. Alice would rather eat rat poison then ask for any help other than a rather vanilla "turn it over to God."

After studying the list of "exact nature" examples, Jim owned up to "always thinking, never feeling." He lived in a never-ending beehive buzz of random thoughts (and, he was sure, very deep thoughts) that never went below his neck. After enough deep digging, Jim admitted that the only thing he ever really felt was the enormous hole in his soul with all the terrible sadness and loneliness that enormous spiritual holes create. That's why he thought he got married—to heal the hole in his soul.

Because neither Alice nor Jim understood or even thought about what makes relationships work (they only thought about what they wanted from the relationship), their marriage was left terribly vulnerable. And what's worse than having something important falling apart right in front of you when you have no idea why it's happening or what you can do about it? (Except, of course, going back to the "tune you know" and hit, hide, or run. And that surely doesn't help.)

MAKE IT REAL

This is a hard patch of ground to cover. I know that. I also know the exquisite pain and misery generated by failing and failed relationships. So it is well worth the effort to dig down, get to the cause, and face the "exact nature" of the obstacles and blind spots that have hurt yourself and others. This kind of hard work generates enormous rewards that will bless your life forever.

ACTION STEPS

Most breakdowns in relationships aren't all that mysterious. And they're not just bad luck, either. When you learn what to look for, the reasons for relationship failure are fairly obvious. Hint: Why does an out-of-shape, unprepared runner fail to win—or even finish—a race?

WRITE: (two or three paragraphs if you can, on the following topics. Give personal examples.)
1. Describe the "exact nature" of your character defect that stands in the way of genuine intimacy.
2. Explain why self-honesty is an important prerequisite to a healthy relationship.

SHARE: (with your group or sponsor)
1. An insight you now have that helps to explain failed relationships in the past.
2. Tell what steps you are taking to prepare yourself to be a better partner in your relationships.

CONSCIOUS CONTACT: Ask your Higher Power for the humility to address your own shortcomings in relationships.

• • •

• WEEK 43 •

Wait at Least a Year

Program wisdom has always advised new (or new again) members not to make any hurried decisions in their lives, *especially around relationships.*

That's no great problem for many of us—unless and until an exciting new relationship appears on the horizon. When that happens, feelings can overtake us. Conventional wisdom about waiting at least a year before making major relationship decisions can quickly go out the window. And more often than not, the results are painful and dangerous to recovery.

As with most things in recovery, no one said this "one-year rule" is easy. (Many recovery sources advise avoiding these decisions for at least *two* years.) However long the right waiting period before getting involved in an exclusive, committed relationship is, the pull toward one shouldn't be surprising. In Week 40, I pointed out that relationships are the most powerful force in our world. Relationships aren't part of who we are. They are *all* of who we are.

Think again of the "exact nature" of our problem (weeks 8 through 10). The problem is not alcohol or drugs. The problem is spiritual bankruptcy, also called the hole in the soul. And at the heart of the hole in the soul, in ever-widening and more powerful ripples, is *isolation.* So what's the answer? What's the solution? Making connections, of course! Forming relationships is the answer. When a recovering person gets halfway well and can think and feel again, *of course* his or her spirit craves all the intimacy it can get. So, like squeezing an orange for every last drop, many of us gallop into a romantic relationship before we're ready and able to function as a healthy partner.

Often, there's an anguished, angry outcry at this point. "But I'm healed! Don't tell me I'm not ready and able to have a relationship!" And for people in this situation, you might as well throw a ping-pong ball at a brick wall for all the difference that conventional wisdom makes.

Why wait? What's the value of the conventional wisdom?

Again, loving is *not* the same thing as making relationships work (weeks 41 and 42). If someone experiences a massive outpouring of emotion fueled by a mad rush to escape loneliness, it does not necessarily mean the person has the *skills* to make a relationship work. No matter how powerful the emotions that add up to feeling "in love," if the skills and maturity aren't there, the love will die like a flower in the first blast of fall's chill air. Then the person looks around, wondering, "How in the heck did I get here? And how do I ever get out?" To say the least, recovery takes a backseat in these situations. And recovery is a jealous lover. If it isn't first, it gets up and leaves.

Successful, lasting relationships are *not* simply a matter of being blown away by overwhelming emotions. For sure, the powerful emotions generated by a new relationship are nice. They're *wonderful*, in fact. The problem is that they don't last unless they're anchored in the necessary skills and abilities that make relationships work.

By far the best form of "relationship insurance" is working your program. And that starts with "me." It's about doing the work recommended throughout this book. It's developing the attitudes that underlie recovery by repeated actions (weeks 16 through 20). It's about getting to the "exact nature of our wrongs" (Week 36) so we don't continue to drag our particular brand of character defects into our new relationships like muddy shoes across a new carpet. It's about staying connected to our Higher Power, self, and others (Week 11) as the primary aid in your toolkit to make the relationship lasting and satisfying.

And as you already know, it takes time, effort, and practice to exchange character defects for character assets. No one in recovery becomes un-selfish, un-afraid, un-compulsive, un-angry, or un-ashamed all at once. *It takes time to develop one's character.* The First Step "moment of clarity" can come in a flash (weeks 8 and 9). But the flash doesn't win the day. What wins the day is being honest, open, and willing *to keep moving* where the God of your understanding is leading you. As we've discussed in this book, the First Step is free. From then on, recovery and freedom must be earned.

So be patient. Give yourself a break. Don't invite failure by jumping into something before you are ready. When you feel the tug of a possible relationship, check it out with your group and sponsor. Take it with you into your Step Eleven prayer. Be silent with it. No matter how compelling and overpowering the urge to "hook up" might be—because "this one is different"—use your tools. Stop before you get so far into the relationship that there's no turning back. Let your head lead your heart on this one. The answer will not be no forever. As you continue to gain time in recovery and continue working the program and developing new skills, you will eventually be ready to form a healthy—and lasting—romantic relationship. Your time will indeed come.

Yes, there are a few exceptions to this rule. There are instances where two people find each other early in their recovery, maybe even in treatment, and form a relationship that endures. *But those are not the rule.* The exception doesn't nullify the rule. Much more often, relationships formed too early play out like Ken and Sandy's.

• • •

Ken and Sandy were, in a way, an unlikely couple. Ken had been sober nearly twenty years. He was deeply involved in the program, sponsored many people along the way, and was always ready to do extraordinary service work. The saying around his group was, "If you want something done, ask Ken to do it." He was the poster boy for the all-around "good guy."

But Ken had never gone far enough in his program (even after twenty years) to get to the "exact nature of his wrongs." Part of his good guy image was built on his overwhelming need to be that good guy. He never said no. He never stood up for himself. It never dawned on him that he had a right to ask others to help him, come to his aid, or stand by him when *he* was in need. In fact, no one ever suspected that Ken ever had a need. He never asked for help, so no one ever offered it to him. As one man in his group said, "If you hit Ken on the head with a hammer, he'd probably tell you how sorry he was for being in your way."

Unlike Ken, Sandy was new to recovery, just three months out of treatment. This was her first stab at living clean and sober. She was sure she "got it." A smart young woman, she was something of a con artist. Her "exact nature" told her that if she could get what she wanted by lying, then only a fool wouldn't lie. Honesty with self and others wasn't her MO. Her "words to live by" were pretty much "What they don't know won't hurt them, or me. So tell them what they want to hear and keep your escape route open."

What she "got" in treatment was that she had to become honest to stay sober. She had to tell the *whole* truth and stay away from any of her usual escape routes. Sandy had been running her whole life. She was habitually petrified of being caught. One of her counselors told her, "You can't be chased if you don't run. So stop doing the things that make it necessary for you to run."

It was great insight. But as I've repeatedly said, *insight isn't change.* Insight is only the first step of change. Knowing is good. But knowing isn't necessarily doing. Knowing she had a knee-jerk tendency to lie and to do whatever it takes to get along didn't mean that Sandy had practiced her recovery values enough to make different choices, choices that would build a new foundation for her life. Knowing only meant that she recognized where the manholes in her life were—the ones she had fallen through so many times.

Flash point: Sandy walked into the meeting Ken regularly attended. After the meeting, they started talking over coffee. The more they talked, the more they found they had in common. (The most important thing they had in common was the hole in the soul, and the loneliness each felt. Why? Because their untended character defects pretty much ruled out either of them enjoying a strong, honest, satisfying relationship.) You know the story. You know how it goes.

A month later, Sandy and Ken moved in together. Two months after that, they were just about killing each other. Sandy was back into her conning, half-truth, "just making sure my ex-boyfriend is okay" dishonest ways. She was shifting back to the left-hand side of the goalposts. Her old habits were kicking the hell out of her fragile new recovery behaviors.

Ken was just miserable. Without his own place, he had nowhere to go where he felt safe. He found it almost impossible to stand up to

Sandy and tell her that what was going on was not okay with him. He was a doormat. And as the saying goes, the only people who value a doormat are those with dirty shoes.

It took an incredible amount of pain for Ken and Sandy to finally get to "enough!" and pull apart. They barely held onto their sobriety. Ken was terribly shamed for "doing such a dumb thing" as getting involved with someone new to recovery when he knew better. Maybe his intellect knew, but the emotional part of him sure didn't (weeks 26 through 30). Sandy admitted the pain but never quite understood what the problem was. She's still sober and in the program, but she's also still puzzled as to what went wrong. (It's the same thing that will go wrong in her next relationship unless she gets to the "exact nature" of her wrongs and learns to stay connected in honest relationship with her Higher Power, self, and others.)

MAKE IT REAL

Yes, this is tough news to swallow, especially if you're falling (or running) into a deep romantic relationship before you're ready. No one wants to hear "Wait!" when their heart so badly wants what it wants. But prematurely leaping into a relationship has led to countless relapses. Go back and read your list from Week 4 to recall what you stand to lose by relapse. Please, *do this critical work*. Failure here, around primary, exclusive relationships, invites incredible pain and suffering into your life. The best way to avoid a landmine blowing up in your face down the line is to not put it out there in the first place.

ACTION STEPS

Of course you want a loving, committed relationship. We all do! But it isn't wise—let alone loving—to invite someone to share your life before you have the skills to make a relationship work. The watchword here is *readiness*.

WRITE: (two or three paragraphs if you can, on the following topics. Give personal examples.)

1. If you were a counselor, what would you tell Ken and Sandy individually and as a couple?
2. As best you can, explain the difference between intellectually knowing something and emotionally knowing it.

SHARE: (with your group or sponsor)

1. Ask old-timers in your group why they think the "one-year rule" is a good idea.
2. Talk about a skill you need to develop before starting a new relationship or trying to restart an old one.

CONSCIOUS CONTACT: Ask your Higher Power for the wisdom to be patient.

REACH OUT: If appropriate, share what you are learning about healthy relationships with your significant other.

•   •   •

• WEEK 44 •

Relationships and Reconciliation

Sooner or later on the recovery journey, the question of reconciliation surfaces. It may be reconciliation with an estranged significant other, disappointed children, or betrayed parents or friends. Attempts at reconciliation are tricky. More than one "ship of recovery" has been sunk over inept efforts to reconnect with loved ones who are still active addicts. When the rules of reconciliation aren't followed, disaster often follows. The good news is that when they *are* followed, some of life's most rewarding experiences become possible. So what are those rules?

Let's first look at three principles that cover all relationships, including relationships we would like to repair. After studying these principles, we'll examine the rules that specifically govern successful attempts at reconciliation.

PRINCIPLE ONE

Every relationship is as healthy (or sick) as *both* people are willing and able to make it. Relationships take both people. You simply cannot heal a relationship by yourself—two is the smallest number needed for this work.

No matter how badly someone wants or needs a relationship to be healed, if *both* parties aren't willing and able to contribute, the relationship cannot be successful and rewarding. There can be no such thing in a relationship as "You have to say yes," or "Be in this relationship or you'll be sorry." Fear and intimidation are exactly the kinds of attitudes that destroy relationships.

PRINCIPLE TWO

Relationships require skills. The skills necessary for healthy relationships (and therefore for reconciliation) are spelled out in Week 41. It's worth repeating, though, that *loving* and *making relationships work* are two different things. Lots of people love who can't make relationships (or reconciliation) work. When thinking about reconciliation, it's important to look at the relationship and ask yourself, "Do both of us have a sufficient skill level to make this thing work?"

PRINCIPLE THREE

The first commitment in making a relationship work is *not* the commitment to the relationship. The first commitment *each* person must make is to developing better relationship skills (Week 41). Since no one has control of another person's decisions, we can only take control of our own readiness.

I've seen many, many people make what looks like a total, 100 percent commitment to a relationship (usually with words like "I really love you!") but then totally drop the ball when asked the question "What is it that *you* must change in yourself to become a more trustworthy partner in this relationship?" Many people are all for the relationship—as long as *they* don't have to change. But "business as usual" doesn't work if that business has so far taken them to the relationship scrap heap.

The above principles will likely be helpful if you feel the need for reconciliation—perhaps as the result of doing Steps Eight and Nine. But even more so, the following rules can work as guideposts over this tricky ground.

RULE ONE

CHECK YOUR ATTITUDE. Remember that relationships and therefore reconciliation can never be owed or demanded. Sometimes people in recovery develop an unhelpful attitude, such as "Look how much work I've done. Look at all the changes I've made. You owe it to me to let me back in your life."

Other recovering people use their new recovery words, phrases, and ideas as shaming tools or "moral prods" to force those they seek reconciliation with to "get with the program." What these people fail to understand or see (which is why a sponsor and an honest group are so important) is that these were the same tactics that likely drove the other away in the first place. When you're being whipped, who cares if the whip is held in the right or the left hand? A whip is a whip.

But if reconciliation is approached with the attitudes and values stated in Week 41 (trust, honesty, humility, commitment, and compromise), well then that is a whole different ballgame. On that foundation a truly beautiful home can be built.

RULE TWO

CHECK YOUR MOTIVE. I've seen situations where the motive for reconciliation is to show the other how much you've grown, to prove your superiority, or to demonstrate your new, beefed-up spirituality. But as they say down South, "That dog won't hunt."

On the other side of this extreme are the folks who desperately seek reconciliation because their value still depends on getting approval from the estranged loved ones. But recovery is all about the emergence of one's *own* sense of self. It's about being who we decide to be regardless of what others may think or say.

Reconciliation cannot be either a siege or waving the white flag of surrender. Successful reconciliation happens when both parties approach each other with healthy attitudes, values, and motives already in place.

RULE THREE

BE REALISTIC. In reconciliation (as well as most other things), expectations are everything. Frustration is always relative to expectation. If the expectations are unrealistic, the level of frustration (which is a slippery slope to relapse) will be exaggerated.

What I am saying is, no matter how much you love those others and want to reconnect with them, if they are not willing *and* able to function in a healthy relationship, reconciliation is not possible.

If they are active addicts or still filled with anger, distrust, or resentments—if the attack dogs around the hole in their soul are on full alert—reconciliation is not possible.

It's a mistake to imagine that just because you've changed, everyone else has, too. You can't even assume that others are particularly happy with the changes you've made. More than one person in recovery has become a threat or a source of guilt to those who are still using. Uneasy with changes, they may even, in many little (or big) ways, try to influence you to once again become "one of the gang."

It's a good exercise to make a list of all those you're thinking of reconciling with. Look at each name through the lens of the attitudes, values, and skills listed above, and rate them on a score of 1 to 10. Then adjust your expectations to the level of attitudes and skills represented.

It is never fair (or a successful ploy) to insist that people give you what they don't have to give.

RULE FOUR

NEVER GO ALONE. Reconciliation is unpredictable and often difficult. Check out your motives and expectations with trusted others. Plan your strategy with other recovering people who may have experience with reconciliation. Work your three "staying connected power sources" (Week 11)—plugged into your Higher Power, self, and others for all you're worth.

If Rule Four seems odd to you—not only *letting* but *inviting* others this deeply into your personal life—then rethink whether you're ready for reconciliation. Perhaps there are too many dark corners in your house of recovery. If you aren't comfortable asking for help, direction, and wisdom from others regarding reconciliation, then you'd best let some light in before running off into the dark.

In one way or another, perhaps physically but always spiritually and emotionally, take your team with you. Let your team know what you are up to. Ask for their advice, support, and prayers or positive thoughts. Have a telephone number you can call during your reconciliation efforts to promptly report success—or to find support if things aren't turning out the way you wanted.

RULE FIVE

PROTECT YOURSELF. As you plan your strategy for reconciliation, make sure you're not physically or spiritually isolated in your attempt. For example, don't get stuck at a family gathering or reunion with no car or a plan to leave if things turn dangerous in one way or another. You have rights, too, and your rights count. You never owe it to anyone to put yourself in a dangerous situation. Nothing is more important than protecting your sobriety.

Remember Rule Four—never go alone. Every step toward recovery and away from active addiction includes staying connected. This is especially true in attempting reconciliation. Let your group and sponsor(s) know what you're doing and how you plan to proceed so they can hold you in prayer as you reach out to heal strained or broken relationships. Set up a "debriefing" call or meeting with someone after your attempt so you can share what happened and what you learned in your efforts. If nothing else, clarifying what you learned can be helpful to share with another who has not been down this path before.

MAKE IT REAL

As the saying goes, "Nothing is quite so dangerous as ignorance in action." It's tempting at times (some would say especially for an addict) to rush off with no forethought or planning on a good-willed attempt to "make things right." A poorly thought-out attempt at reconciliation can be devastating. So, if reconciliation is on your recovery to-do list, *do this work*. Think it out. Follow the rules. Do it right to give yourself the best chance of success—no matter what happens.

ACTION STEPS

Strained relationships are a source of great anxiety for newly recovering people. We often try to mend fences without enough thought or preparation. If you sincerely want a good result—instead of merely relief from guilt or embarrassment—think through your efforts with trusted others.

WRITE: (two or three paragraphs if you can, on the following topics. Give personal examples.)
1. Describe the most important "reconciliation situations" in your life (partner, children, or parents, for example).
2. Thinking of the principles and rules in this week's reading, what's the lesson about reconciliation?

SHARE: (with your group or sponsor)
1. Explain your main reasons for wanting to reconcile.
2. In what ways are you increasing your own relationship skills level? Give examples.

CONSCIOUS CONTACT: Ask your Higher Power for help in aligning your motives and expectations with program wisdom.

• • •

Spirituality

• WEEK 45 •

Spirituality: Trusting the Front Door

Some of you working through this book may wonder, "Why are we back to spirituality? I thought we already covered that!"

Here's why: The primary element woven through all these weeks is this: *There is no spiritual side of recovery. It is all spiritual.* Which raises this question: What is your understanding of spirituality?

Many, probably most, people think of spirituality as certain things a person *does*. Some acts are spiritual and some aren't. Really spiritual people, so this line of thinking goes, are those who do a lot of those spiritual acts—such as praying, meditating, having spiritual awakenings, making conscious contact with the God of their understanding. "Doing" is certainly a part of spirituality.

But the spirituality I'm talking about isn't about one act being spiritual and another one not. What I'm talking about is the *intention and attitude* that penetrates and permeates *all* of one's life. In this line of thinking, spirituality isn't what we do; it is *who we are*. In this line of thinking, there is no such thing as a thought, word, or deed that is not and cannot be spiritual.

Dennis, a dear friend of mine, was into his sixth month of treatment when he told me about his new work assignment for the next three months. His job was to clean all the toilets in the large treatment facility. Deeply caught up in the spirit of recovery and total surrender to his Higher Power, Dennis said with a flourish—everything Dennis does is with a flourish—"It doesn't matter what job they give me. I feel that every job comes from God. If they want me to clean the toilets, I'll be the best toilet cleaner they ever had. I'll do the work to the best of my ability and use it as an act of gratitude for what God and recovery have given me."

Most people wouldn't think of cleaning toilets as a spiritual act, but Dennis did. It isn't the *what* that counts in spirituality, it's the *why*. It's about bringing trust, humility, and honesty into *everything* we do (as the Twelfth Step says, "in all our affairs"). Which brings us to an all-important spiritual question: Can we trust that something so good is coming in the front door that we're willing to give up all our back doors?

FRONT DOORS AND BACK DOORS

Back doors don't work. The only place back doors lead to is the dark alley of relapse and misery. Happy is the person who has learned (many would say *finally* learned) to trust that what is coming through the front door of recovery will be infinitely better than anything that could possibly be gained by keeping an "escape route" open through the back door.

Your recovery is as good as the honesty you practice. Honesty (Week 16) is a key ingredient of staying connected. And the spiritual firepower gained from staying connected is the *only* power strong enough to arrest an addiction and lead you to the true joy, serenity, and peace of mind that comes through ongoing recovery. Again, that is why the very last truth spoken in the Steps is we "practice these principles in *all* our affairs."

Practicing the principles of recovery leaves no wiggle room. The principles advise us that "all it takes is all there is." This means no back doors. No protected escape routes left to rabbit through. No hidey-holes shielded from the light that recovery is. No secret corners too dark for honesty and surrender. All it takes is *all* there is.

What kind of back doors? Here are some oldies but goodies that were mentioned in a class I recently taught:

- that one last resentment I *will not* let go of
- that one hidden character defect I have not yet "become willing" to face or surrender
- that one last boyfriend or girlfriend who has nothing to do with going forward in recovery and everything to do with

going back to the old ways—the way of life I'm not quite willing to move away from "just in case this 'recovery thing' doesn't pan out"

- that best friend from the old using days I'm not ready to cut ties with
- "just once in a while" going to the club where I know my sobriety is at great risk
- that last malignant tumor of guilt and shame I'm not ready to surrender to self-forgiveness
- that terrible secret fear I have of ever really trusting anyone, including God
- that tenacious inner belief that the only way anyone, including God, would want me around is if I earn that acceptance by superhuman volunteering or service work
- the abiding sense that I must be (but can't be) perfect—that surely I'm not really doing this "recovery thing" well enough to make it work
- that last hidden piece (whatever it is) that I'm still withholding from "let go and let God"

Do you have others you would add to this list?

Clearly, none of us is perfect. Recovery is a process. No one "does recovery" all at once. There is no such thing in recovery as, "Okay, I did it. Now I'm done." No one can say it's easy to give up your back door. But what anyone in quality recovery will tell you is that along the way, little by little, sometimes—but not usually—in white-hot hits of spirituality, back doors must be surrendered in favor of the glory awaiting entry through the front door.

Spirituality is all about *attitude*. It's about how we choose to live our lives, one day at a time. It's about the integrity we bring to the thousand and one decisions we make each day. It's not just a collection of spiritual acts we try to stack up along the way. "Spirituality" means the attitude, courage, and commitment we bring to the table each day of our lives—no matter what siren song our addiction might be singing. Ultimately, spirituality is the magic carpet that takes a person who once was "tore up from the floor up" all the way up to touch the face of the God of his or her understanding.

Life doesn't get any more spiritual than trusting the good coming to us through the front door of recovery *enough*—enough to surrender our hidey-holes and back doors.

MAKE IT REAL

Spirituality is where all the action is. Spirituality is where recovery happens. Living a spiritual life takes commitment and willingness to work at it. But think about what's at stake for an alcoholic/addict in recovery! Looking at (or for) your back doors is a very useful exercise for people in recovery. It's more than worthy of your time and attention to take the following work seriously.

ACTION STEPS

True spirituality isn't about being prim, proper, or pious. Rather, it's about being honest and humble in "all our affairs." It's about the integrity that comes from working the Steps, one day at a time.

WRITE: (two or three paragraphs if you can, on the following topics. Give personal examples.)
1. Explain the meaning of "front doors" and "back doors" in recovery. Give examples.
2. Name and describe one or two "back doors" you've used and not yet given up.

SHARE: (with your group or sponsor)
1. Tell what you're going to do about a resentment or character defect you've still not surrendered.
2. Explain the difference between "spiritual acts" and "spiritual living."

CONSCIOUS CONTACT: Thank your Higher Power for the gains you've made so far. Ask for continuing support.

• • •

• WEEK 46 •

Spirituality Must Go through Our Humanity

Last week's work established that spirituality is not just a *part* of your recovery life but the *actual fabric* of your recovering life. This week's lesson is a natural next step. If spirituality is the fabric of your life, then of course it has to run through, affect, concern itself, and take issue with who you are as you live your life on life's terms.

But that "of course" isn't always so apparent. If you, knowingly or not, see spirituality as certain acts you do, that leaves a whole lot of life that isn't covered by those acts. That's how so-called spiritual people can end up so full of self, fear, and anger. And that's how people who may never stop talking about spirituality can also be hostile, judgmental, and uninterested in down-and-dirty service work. It's not uncommon to find some in recovery who declare themselves "spiritual people" but fail to greet the new person or go out of their way to help a brother or sister in need.

The point is this: Spirituality that does not go through our humanity—that does not become who we are—ends up in a kind of idolatry before the program's forgiving God of second chances.

THE DOOR TO SPIRITUALITY

Last week, we talked about the need to give up the back doors that lead to potential relapse and to instead walk through the front door into a life of recovery. This week, we're going to think of spirituality as a door. Doors can be open or they can be closed. When a door is closed, there's no access to whatever is behind it. The only way to reach what's behind the door—or for whatever is back there to get to you—is to *open the door.*

All recovering alcoholics/addicts, whether dually addicted or not, tend to want the door to spirituality kept closed. Why? So whatever is behind the door doesn't come out and attack them! Behind that door is all the pain, guilt, fear, rage, and shame of living under the boot heel of active addiction. Behind that door is the yellow-eyed wolf of a life lived in a dark cave for many lost years. No small part of active addiction's power comes from the desperate inner need to stay in denial and *keep that damn door shut!*

Yet behind that same door is the angel of recovery. Behind that door is also where grace, light, and freedom are to be found. To embrace and be embraced by this angel of recovery, you must be willing to open that door of spirituality (one step at a time, one day at a time). *To find the angel, you must be willing to face your wolf.*

Some would say, "Well, that's bad news!" But others have found that opening that door is nothing but good news. In fact, it's the best news you can imagine. One reason is that no one has to take—or can take—this fearsome step alone. As you stay connected to your Higher Power, self, and others, you make the awesome discovery that the angel trumps the wolf. You realize at last that there's no secret, fear, shame, or guilt that cannot be put in its place. Perhaps for the first time you see that there's no need to be perfect or even to try to be perfect. Because you are *already* far more than acceptable and worthy. In fact, you are loved—just the way you are.

Those who stay connected and thereby allow their spirituality to run *through* their humanity increasingly "come to believe" that their Higher Power uses them—not in spite of what they have done or where they have been, but *because* of what they have done and where they have been. Holding this pain up to the power and grace of recovery opens the door and gives them access to their own inner depths and also to others. As clearly as they see their own image in a mirror, they come to recognize that their whole lives, no matter what is behind the closed door, have been preparation for the grand work they are now called to do.

WE ARE CHAMPIONS

A consistent high point of my week is the class I teach at the Salvation Army. We always start with the same two points. Imagine me like a berserk cheerleader shouting out to the hundred or so men in the class, "What is point one?" They shout back, "We never have to use again!" "And the second point?" I shout back at them. They respond, "We have a purpose. God will use us to do work no one else can do as well as we can."

I don't know how much the men get out of the rest of the class. That isn't up to me. It's up to them and the God of their understanding. But I know very well that they really get behind shouting that they *can indeed* arrest their addiction and professing that their lives have meaning and purpose *because* of who they are and what they have done. The profession of those two truths goes "all the way down," as the men say, to the deepest part of what lies behind their door. Or at least as deep as they are willing and able to let it go at that moment.

We end our class in the same manner. I learned this from watching Abe, who had a forty-six-year-long addiction to heroin. (He has now been clean and sober for more than a year and is a Twelve Step warrior of the finest kind.) We were doing a class together at a prison. Abe told the men he had spent twenty-four years there—five of those years in solitary confinement. But now he knows a better way. With a fervor and intensity that only comes from "having been there," he went on to tell the inmates, "You are champions. *You are champions.*" The goodness of this man and the power of grace to change lives—no matter how damaged they had been—brought tears to my eyes and sent a chill up my back. Abe had given me another fine gift. And since gifts are to be used, I end each class by shouting out to my men, "You are CHAMPIONS!" We've done it enough now that they know what to do. I then shout out this question, "Who are you?" As one they roar back, "We are CHAMPIONS!" Then I ask them a second and a third time, "Who are you?" By that time the place is rocking.

Some may think this exercise is hokey or overly emotional. But for men who have pretty much lived behind a closed door all their lives, it's like spring coming after winter. Most have never been told they were champions or ever thought about themselves in any positive way. Most had given up on sobriety, let alone any kind of spiritual life. But here they are, enthusiastically encouraged to see themselves as winners, to claim that they are champions, to open the door and embrace the angel who awaits them there—as well as face the wolf of whatever they have done (or had been done to them) during their long winter. If they keep their door open and stay connected, the wolf doesn't stand a chance against the angel.

Over the decades, I've discovered there are lots of folks besides felons and "low-bottom drunks" who need to know *they are champions.* We all are.

MAKE IT REAL

Are you one of those who finds being loved far more uncomfortable than staying isolated? In spite of the bloated ego sitting on top of your self-contempt, do you believe you are a champion? Have you kept your door closed to spirituality because you're afraid of the wolf of your past—but then also missed the presence of the recovery angel waiting for you there? If your answer is yes, be sure to *do this work.* You have no idea of the freedom and joy that waits for you just behind the door.

ACTION STEPS

Your spirituality is based on acceptance of yourself—warts and all. Spirituality doesn't float somewhere high above your humanity and your history. It embraces and engulfs all of you. So open the door and enter the Fellowship.

WRITE: (two or three paragraphs if you can, on the following topics. Give personal examples.)

1. Describe something you've kept hidden behind a closed door in your mind.
2. Explain why opening the door is both good news and bad news.

SHARE: (with your group or sponsor)
1. Thank your sponsor for his or her willingness to share honestly.
2. Reveal a persistent inner feeling that you've never shared with anyone.

CONSCIOUS CONTACT: Ask your Higher Power's help in becoming honest, open, and willing.

● ● ●

• WEEK 47 •

Spirituality: You Are Welcome Here

Recovery is filled with discovery. One of the most important discoveries is finding that you are *welcome*. So welcome back into your own life as well as into the lives of your fellows and into the presence of your Higher Power, who never left you in the first place. (You were never lost even though you may have felt like it. Your Higher Power always knew where you were.)

My goal in this last section is to express how spirituality is the foundation we stand on—the way we live and not just the spiritual acts we might do. As we go from the problem to the solution and then on to all aspects of working the solution (weeks 4 through 52), this topic of "welcome" stands at the heart of the Promises' blessings. Recovery, the solution, is all about moving from isolation to welcome.

Let me share with you a most beautiful event I witnessed that perfectly expressed the treasure of being welcome. On its surface, I guess some could say, "Oh, that isn't really a Twelve Step story." But the inner meaning of the story says everything that's important about the spiritual essence of recovery.

I've mentioned that I attend a church that has many members who are in recovery. Some would say our church is just an extension of the Eleventh Step. It's a place of honesty, healing, and connection, "all the way down," coming from behind the pried-open doors of our lives to the God of second chances. The lesson given me about the significance of "you are welcome here" happened like this:

Brenda is the gifted soloist at my church. She has that special and rare gift of music that creates an immediate soul connection with those who hear her song. For me nothing goes quite so deep as when she sings, "You are welcome here." To me, it feels like a silky net thrown out to draw us all closer together at one table.

I asked her about it once, and she told me it wasn't really a song, but just "something she made up." She said it jumped from her spirit to her lips—and then out to us. That made sense to me because the whole "song" is only four words long. It's just the line "You are welcome here." Brenda sings it over and over again—maybe a dozen times. She doesn't just stand still and sing. Or stand in a place where the choir or the song leader is supposed to stand. Our church isn't like that. No, as she sings the words, she moves around, up and down the aisles, looking into people's eyes. She's really *telling* us, "You are welcome here." She's *inviting* us to step up and accept that invitation— again, no matter where we've been or what we might have done in our lost years (and most of us have done plenty). Our church is all about starting over, no matter what. It's about discovering that we are welcome at last—not just tolerated or "put up with." And that journey started by crawling on our hands and knees through the low door of brokenness—which is the straight road to conscious contact with a Higher Power, "who would and could if he were sought."

One Sunday, Ruby was sitting in the first chair of the first row on the aisle that Brenda uses as a launching pad. Ruby is a special woman. I guess she's in her thirties, and she's obviously mentally and physically impaired. But not so impaired she can't get up, rock to the music, and turn on a million-watt smile. And she isn't so impaired that she doesn't know the great significance of the invitation. Ruby totally understands what Brenda is singing about.

On this given Sunday, as Brenda moved up and down and across the aisles seeking those who looked especially in need of knowing "you are welcome here," she caught Ruby's eye. The magic was on. *Welcome* means fellowship. It means, "The door is open here. You are safe." It means, "You are most welcome to come as you are, but you won't leave as you came."

With her free hand, Brenda reached out to Ruby as she held the mike with the other. They held hands. No one else in the church existed for them as Ruby felt the full force of the power coming through Brenda. Now all the people there were clapping, singing, being lifted up by the beautiful communication taking place between the two women.

I suspect there were many, many times in Ruby's life when she did *not* feel welcome. Our world (thank God not the world of recovery!) has precious little time for the slow, the halt, or the lame. "Precious" is often in short supply. But that's exactly what Brenda was telling Ruby. She was telling her that she was precious, and no matter what the sightless don't see, Brenda saw it. Brenda knew the truth about Ruby.

I was sitting at an angle where I could see both women. Have you, dear reader and fellow traveler on the recovery road, had the honor and privilege of seeing, or better yet, playing a part in another's spiritual awakening (or best of all, your own)? Then you know what I'm talking about but can never adequately explain. Ruby's face *glowed* the whole time Brenda wrapped her in song like a soft blanket. Perhaps Ruby's "impediment" was a gift in the sense that it freed her to fully express the truth of her joy that so many of us "normal" people are inclined to hide or tone down.

Brenda would say that God set the table. Her job was just to invite others to come in and be fed. Ruby knew full well she was welcome. She went away full.

I once asked Brenda what kind of welcome she was singing about. Are we welcoming God into our life? Is God beckoning us to draw near and increase our "conscious connection"? Was her song telling us that we all are welcome into each other's lives? That indeed we are a family offering each other hope and strength as long as we stay connected? "Who is welcome where?" I asked her.

She just looked at me like a teacher working with a slow student. "All of it," she said. "Any of it. It's whatever you need it to be whenever you hear it." End of story.

But for many of us, it's not the end of the story. It's the start of the story, the beginning of the journey. We've reached the point in our spirituality where the question of whether or not we can accept that we are welcome becomes the tipping point. It's the crossroads where (at least for now) we decide to let the door stay open and welcome the angel of recovery or (at least for now) shy away from what's behind the open door because it seems too much to deal with—both the beautiful and the terrifying. So we stop for a bit and take a rest. Which is okay.

Recovery is a process. It surges ahead one day at a time, sometimes inch by inch. The important question is not where we are on the road—it's the direction we're going. None of us will ever "get there." There is no *place* to get to. "There" is right now and it's right here. As long as we're trying to accept that "You are welcome here," we are going in the right direction. As long as we surround ourselves with people who reflect back to us that we are important, clean, worthy, and welcome, then we are on our way and all is well with our world.

Listen hard with the ears of your spirit. Maybe you can hear Brenda telling you how welcome you are to be here. I hope so.

MAKE IT REAL

Loving is easy for most of us. Accepting that we are loved is far more dangerous and difficult. Welcoming others may come easy to us. Allowing ourselves to be welcomed is a stumbling block for many. So the work of this week is vitally important. Doing it is well worth the effort.

ACTION STEPS

Today is not yesterday. Now is not then. It would be a terrible mistake to allow "what was" to contaminate our bright new "what is." Today the news is nothing but good. As Paul Simon said in his beautiful song, "We all will be received in Graceland."

WRITE: (two or three paragraphs if you can, on the following topics. Give personal examples.)
1. If you find it easier to love others than yourself, list two or three "learned lies" that make you feel unworthy.
2. List three behaviors you can do to become more like Ruby— or Brenda.

SHARE: (with your group or sponsor)
1. Specific details of your plan to rehabilitate your own self-image.
2. Your appreciation and gratitude for the welcoming words and actions of people in the Fellowship.

CONSCIOUS CONTACT: Ask your Higher Power to help you turn away from the past so you can enjoy the sunshine of today.

REACH OUT: Make it a daily practice to smile at people, compliment them, and encourage them. (We all need it.)

● ● ●

• WEEK 48 •

Spirituality: As One Day at a Time

I met up with Sophie Jo last week. At sixteen months into her recovery, she's not a happy camper. What was eating her lunch? She was sure she wasn't going fast enough or far enough in her recovery. Her complaint was, "Everyone seems to be doing so much better than me." She talked about others (seemingly) having so much more serenity and joy than she did. Sophie said she felt like a total loser.

The standard response from a program sponsor or coach, of course, is to lay on old program wisdom such as "Take it a day at a time," "Easy does it," or maybe suggest curbing your ego in imagining you should be so much further along. Or maybe not.

I've found that recovery is and always will be a one-on-one proposition. Most often, the best way to help someone else is by listening closely—listening to who they are and what they are trying to communicate. Sometimes laying on "old program wisdom," no matter how tried and true, just isn't the best way to go if you're trying to make a heart connection. So it was in Sophie's case.

Like many women in recovery, Sophie had sustained deep and grievous wounds from her childhood on. The men in her life, whose sacred job it was to protect and teach her, had turned on her in the worst possible manner. Early on, Sophie learned that the quickest way to numb the pain was through alcohol and drugs. And that's what she did for nearly thirty years—right up to the past sixteen months. During all those lost years, she acted out what the men in her life had told her she was worth. Her abiding sense of self was that she was "dirty."

Sophie had never heard of childhood onset PTSD or dual diagnosis (Week 3). But as the saying goes, if you looked up childhood onset PTSD in the dictionary, you'd find her picture there. When I told her that, she said, "No, you wouldn't. I don't even know what that means. I'll tell you where you'd find my picture—under 'crazy, dirty bitch.'"

Sophie Jo really is a miracle of the power of recovery. Somehow, through all the trauma and betrayal—first done to her by others, then done to her by herself—she retained an amazing capacity to love others. She found it impossible to see another human being in pain and not go to any length to relieve that person's suffering. Her demon was also her angel.

She said her problem was lack of spirituality—that she just wasn't a good enough person to receive the great gift of recovery. I told her that I, too, thought her problem was spirituality—but it was not that she wasn't good enough. *The problem was that she couldn't accept just how truly good and brave she was.* Again, she brought up the whole "dirty" thing. "No," I said. "All the tragic things that happened to you, and all that you did to yourself in your 'lost years,' was just your pain acting out. All of that is about *then*. But your recovery is about *now*—and in the now you shine as clean and bright as a shiny new penny."

Sophie had no idea of how well she was doing. She had no idea of how brave and noble her efforts were. Even though the wolf behind her door was as big and mean as a wounded bear, Sophie—with her threefold connection to her Higher Power, self, and others wrapped around her like a warm blanket—had opened that door and was "entirely willing" to face whatever waited there.

The wolf didn't scare Sophie Jo. She knew all about the wolf. She'd lived with the wolf her whole life. What scared her silly was the angel who was also waiting for her. As I've said so many times in these weeks, loving isn't the hard part. Accepting that we *are* loved is what so often knocks us out. That's where the guard dogs are on patrol—preventing us from accepting that we *are* acceptable, *are* worthy, *are* lovable, and, mostly, are forgiven by everyone—except ourselves.

The point is not to give up. *Never give up*, no matter how slow your growth seems or how far you think you're lagging behind others. The point is, no matter how you feel, to keep pressing on. Few of us have any real sense of the nobility of our recovery journey.

Here's a quote from a letter I received recently. It's all about Sophie Jo and everyone like her in recovery who finds it difficult to own and celebrate what a splendid job they are doing with their lives. See if you can guess where the letter came from.

It reads:

> You mentioned that many people you come across in recovery have no clue as to the meaning of trust, fellowship, or being vulnerable. Those are tough concepts to teach people whose armor is welded on. And actually, "coax to accept" is probably a better phrase than "teach."
>
> Vulnerability is such a double-edged sword! On the one hand, being vulnerable enough to put yourself out there is the only way to fully experience life, making things that much richer and rewarding—or that much more painful and devastating. By the same token, armoring yourself against the world may protect you from a lot of hurts, but you can't dance in a suit of armor, or feel a sensual touch on your skin, or swim without sinking. It's a question of experiencing life and all it has to offer, good and bad—or merely existing instead of living.

So where do you think this letter came from? A seminary, maybe? Or a ministry school? Maybe from a psychology student?

No, it came from a young man serving a life sentence for murdering two people. He entered prison at eighteen and now is in the twenty-fifth year of his sentence. John has been drug and alcohol free for years, but he may never live a single day outside prison walls. Yet the beauty of his spirit is awesome. Prison walls are no match for grace. Neither is a life like Sophie Jo's, which has been so full of tears and sorrow. Nothing can stop the power of recovery built on a foundation that is honest, open, and willing—and fueled by staying connected to our Higher Power, self, and others.

Whose journey is nobler—those who seem to have an easier time moving through the stages of recovery (although who can say what's going on inside of anyone else?) or those who must struggle so hard for every inch of progress? Easy or hard, it doesn't matter. Recovery is not a competition. The only thing that matters is that you respond as best you can (and that is never perfectly) to the call you've heard. Everyone in recovery has been summoned to travel a higher road. In response to the gift of that summons, we are all called to go as far as we can, as best we can, for as long as we can.

Whether your name is Brenda or Ruby, Sophie Jo or John, Bill W. or Dr. Bob—the rewards are there for all of us. The Promises are there for all of us. If we just push on through and keep going, no matter how rough the road may be at times, we will discover that what was once terrifying and difficult is now a source of comfort and joy. And in fact, we wouldn't trade it for anything on this earth. What we've found is precious, and we will protect and defend it from anything that would steal it away from us.

And to you, Sophie Jo, I say this: Just keep coming. One of these days, you will look in the mirror, and the beauty of what you see will knock your socks off.

MAKE IT REAL

For some, this whole section on spirituality-as-life is difficult. They're still more comfortable seeing themselves as they were "then"—before answering their call to recovery. But do this work anyway. Keep at it until the face you see in the mirror is one you are not loath to look at. Far from it. Keep at it until you see the face of someone you're proud of. *Please,* do this work. Someone around you needs the depth and wisdom you will gain by doing this work.

ACTION STEPS

Most of us have to do a *lot* of changing before our self-image changes. We've discounted and berated ourselves for so long that we're simply unable to do an accurate self-assessment. So forget about judging or comparing yourself to others. If you're doing the best you can, one day at a time, you're doing fine!

WRITE: (two or three paragraphs if you can, on the following topics. Give personal examples.)
1. List three of the worst names you call yourself or critical self-descriptions that habitually surface in your mind.
2. If your best friend admitted to having the same unflattering thoughts, what would you say in response?

SHARE: (with your group or sponsor)
1. Ask for help in dealing with any tendency you have to compare your progress with others.
2. Thank your trusted others for their support as you recover self-respect.

CONSCIOUS CONTACT: Ask your Higher Power for the ability to love and forgive yourself.

REACH OUT: After a meeting, tell someone who seems to be losing heart that he or she is doing great.

• • •

• WEEK 49 •

Spirituality as Power

Power is tricky. Why? Because it can be either creative or destructive. A crackling blaze in the fireplace on a cold winter evening is delightful. But that same fire spreading out from a faulty electrical connection next to the drapes is obviously a totally different thing.

Spirituality is the greatest power on earth. It has enough energy to pull life back from the hands of death. Every alcoholic/addict who's made the transition from active addiction to a life in recovery knows this power from an up-close and personal perspective. Personal experience is the best proof of anything, isn't it? *Recovery* is just another word to express the truth of the power of spirituality.

Since experience is the most convincing proof, I'd like to share some real-life examples of this power in action—to go along with the glory of your own story.

• • •

The chaplain at a workhouse got a request from his pal who was the pastor of a large congregation. The pastor knew the chaplain had the rare gift of making people feel loved, especially the men he called "my guys," who were inmates serving out the last year of a longer sentence or sentenced to less than a year. It was September, National Recovery Month, when the pastor asked the chaplain to help show his congregation what recovery was all about by bringing some of "his guys" and "putting on a skit or something."

So on the given Sunday, the chaplain and six men showed up, intending to act out an event that had happened at the workhouse chapel. One of the inmates there, now released, had prayed for "battle angels" to stand on the front porch of his house. Why? He wanted them to guard the front door to keep out the evil forces that were trying to get in while he was away.

The chaplain stood behind the altar that sat on a riser a foot or so above the floor. After explaining the scenario, he called out, "Big Sam!" Sam was in his late twenties, stood six foot four, and weighed maybe 220 pounds. The expression on his face was frightening. He looked like a white, skinhead gang member. He wore one of those muscle shirts (which he didn't want to do, but the chaplain said he needed it to make the point). Sam's massive left arm was totally covered from shoulder to wrist with red, blue, and black tattoos. He called it his "devil arm." Staring out from the jungle of tattoos were skulls, devils' heads, crossed bones, and other images. As Sam crossed his arms and gave the congregation his "street look," every mother in the room pulled her children closer.

Then the chaplain laughed right out loud. It wasn't part of the skit as far as Sam knew, but he kept his glowering look firmly in place. The chaplain then said, "Sam, come up here a minute." Sam was confused—but since the chaplain was his spiritual guide, sponsor, and trusted friend, he turned and walked up to the altar.

"Oh, you look so tough!" the chaplain said. Then he drew the young man close, pulled his head down a bit, and gave him a big kiss on the side of his head. "Now" the chaplain said, "go back and look tough again."

The glory of the story was that when Sam got kissed, his face dissolved into an expression that was as soft and loving and undevillike as imaginable. Pretty amazing, since, as the chaplain knew, Sam didn't have to act to play his "scary street guy" part. With his smile, all the mothers in the church breathed easier. Whether or not the congregation knew it, they had just witnessed the inner beating heart of recovery.

That is the power of spirituality.

● ● ●

At forty-three, Ed got into recovery five years before his wife, Jennifer. As many people in recovery could tell you, those five years were anything but smooth sailing for the couple. It was a blessing to Ed that he became a "double winner" early in that period—meaning he joined Al-Anon as well as staying firmly planted in his AA home group. Al-Anon taught him to detach while keeping solidly on his AA square.

Jennifer's foundation was much more broken than Ed's. As she started using the pry bar of honesty to leverage open the locked door of her life, terrible memories and cries of self-incrimination rushed out at her. The wolves waiting to escape from behind locked doors can be the stuff of nightmares for some. But to her infinite credit, Jennifer kept at it. She stayed connected, and so did Ed.

At one point during her second year of recovery, Ed asked Jennifer to repeat after him, "I am beautiful in your eyes." Ed knew that it was well beyond Jennifer to see her own beauty at this point, but he thought maybe she could admit that she was beautiful in *his* eyes. He was wrong—she wasn't ready yet. She just couldn't make herself say the words. They stuck in her throat like fishhooks.

Then on her fourth recovery birthday, while they celebrated with other friends in the program, Jennifer leaned close to Ed and said the loveliest words Ed had ever heard. She, this woman he truly loved, told him, "Okay, I am beautiful in your eyes. I admit it. I own it. I am thankful."

That is the power of spirituality.

• • •

One Christmas Eve, Karen struck and killed a father and husband while driving under the influence. For that, she got six years in prison. But in terms of regret, guilt, and shame, she got a lifetime sentence.

She is now seven years clean and sober. At the top of her Eighth Step list of amends was the family of the man she killed. Karen knew deep inside herself that if she didn't make this amend, she would never be able to grant herself any level of forgiveness.

About her fifth year in recovery, Karen's "still, small voice" began barking. She was far enough along that she needed to *do something* about this amend. But what? She didn't know where the man's family lived or how to contact them. What she did become aware of, how-ever, was an upcoming regional meeting of MADD (Mothers Against

Drunk Driving) in her area. It was then, she says, that her still, small voice turned into a Marine drill instructor. It became clear to her that she needed to go to that regional meeting, no matter how many were in the hall, get up in front of them all, and say how sorry she was for what she had done.

First of all, she fortified herself. No one in the program recommends going alone. Alone is isolation. Alone is death. So Karen leaned on her connections. She worked her Eleventh Step harder than she ever had. She called on the strength of her sponsor and special group mates. On the day of the convention, her group went with her. Beforehand, many had told her she didn't *have* to do what she was planning. They thought her plan was too extreme. But Karen said, "No, what was extreme was what I did to that man and his family. What I'm doing here is what needs to be done. I made the mess; I can't undo it, but I need to clean it up."

And so she did. At the open mike part of the program, she told the big gathering who she was and what she had done. She asked for their forgiveness and told them that all she could do from here on out was to stay clean and sober and help anyone she could to embrace recovery.

There was some shuffling of feet and murmuring as the crowd listened to Karen. But there was no outrage. No throwing of stones (which Karen half jokingly said wouldn't have surprised her). After making her amends, she walked out of the auditorium with her group, a freer person than when she walked in.

That is the power of spirituality.

• • •

After speaking at an alumni event for a local treatment center, I was standing by the cafeteria as attendees filed in for lunch. One of those who passed by was a woman in her late seventies or eighties. She said her name was Flo and that she'd been in recovery thirty-seven years. Her wrinkled face shone with that wonderful spiritual light some people in long recovery attain. She said she wanted to tell me about her husband, Herb, who had passed the year before.

Herb had come into the program three years before she did. For years before that, they had done a lot of drinking and "carrying on."

Ugly stuff, she said. But once in recovery, neither one of them had ever relapsed. "I guess we realized that what we had was just too good to throw away," she said. Then, with tears brimming in her eyes, she said, "When I knew Herb was getting ready to leave, I climbed in bed with him. I held his arm up since he couldn't lift it himself. I told him, 'Herb, my dear, we won! *You* won. You are moving on sober and loving the Lord.'"

Spirituality is all about winning. In fact, it's the only winning that counts. Flo was right. She and Herb had indeed won.

That is the power of spirituality.

MAKE IT REAL

Reflect on this topic. What is spirituality to you? What does it do? What difference is made by its presence or lack of presence? Where have you seen its sweet face looking out at you? Where have you seen it work miracles? (If you don't take the time to reflect, you never know what you know.) So give this piece of work a dime, and it will give you back a thousand dollars.

ACTION STEPS

In worldly terms, *power* suggests great wealth, status, or authority. But the power of spirituality is truly much greater. Even the most powerful king or business tycoon can't rescue precious lives from the death grip of addiction.

WRITE: (two or three paragraphs if you can, on the following topics. Give personal examples.)

1. Give an example of high-level spirituality you've seen in someone in recovery.
2. In the example you gave above, what was the lesson for you?

SHARE: (with your group or sponsor)
1. Give an example of how your spirituality has grown during your time in recovery.
2. Ask your sponsor to suggest an action you might take to further develop your spirituality.

CONSCIOUS CONTACT: Ask your Higher Power for the wisdom to keep your priorities in order.

• • •

The Great Endeavor: Moving from Self-Contempt to Self-Compassion

• WEEK 50 •

Self-Forgiveness: "If You Won't Forgive Me, Dig a Grave for Two"

So we come to the last weeks of our program. I called this section the "Great Endeavor" because that is what recovery, especially when fully embraced, truly is. *Recovery is change pushed all the way to true transformation.* And the transformation of a human life from loss, sickness, and self-absorption to one of gift, grace, and fellowship is the greatest endeavor a human being can experience or witness. To move from self-contempt to self-compassion encompasses every good thing this life has to offer. For many who have made this leap (with the help of their Higher Power), the first step was granting themselves the mercy of forgiveness. So let's begin right there—with forgiving yourself.

Everyone makes mistakes—that's part of being human. The greater error is not learning from our mistakes. If we learn the lessons that our mistakes produce, the mistakes are not wasted—no matter how grievous they are. If we learn from them, in fact, our mistakes slip over into the "win" column of life. It makes sense, then, that we would forgive ourselves for our wrongdoings that eventually lead to growth, but this is rarely a natural act.

The opposite of forgiving oneself takes many forms, such as resentment, regret, or guilt and shame. Whatever form it takes, not forgiving ourselves creates self-contempt. The problem is that self-contempt and becoming your own best friend—a key to lasting recovery—are mutually exclusive. Refusal to forgive oneself is a terrible waste of life.

It's odd how so many of us freely grant forgiveness to others but refuse to give that gift to ourselves. The distance between the two is a good measure of just what kind of a friend we are to ourselves. Have you heard the saying "If we treated others the way we treat ourselves, we'd be in prison"? It's true enough. For some misguided reason, many of us habitually judge the wrongs and mistakes *we* make as far worse than the decisions made by others. When it comes to guilt and relentless self-recrimination, many of us believe to the bottom of our souls that we are the worst of the worst.

Do any of the following real-life examples feel or sound familiar?

● ● ●

Angela is not only an addict, but she also married an active alcoholic. Maybe she should have known better, but she didn't. Only nineteen when she married, and heading into her own addiction, she had a limited life experience and didn't know herself very well yet. She found recovery but stayed in that relationship for more than twenty years. With the hindsight of time and the blessing of Al-Anon, she now has a much better understanding of why she married "her alcoholic" and why she stayed so long in the relationship that was killing her spirit.

Understanding often brings with it a wave of forgiveness. Angela, however, was unable to forgive herself. Her problem wasn't about feeling she "wasted her life," but rather was about what she had modeled for her son and daughter. Her son is an active addict, and her beloved daughter married as her mother did, teaming up with an addict. No matter how much Angela understood about the disease of addiction and the harm it does the family, she found it impossible to forgive herself, as she says, for what she believes she did to her kids by staying.

But then the light went on. She came to understand that beating up on herself wasn't virtue, nor was it asked of her by her program. It was just her lousy way of making up to anyone, including herself, for the hell of staying put all those years.

Working with her sponsor and a gifted therapist, she got to the bottom of her need to punish herself (which she was practicing long before she crossed over into her addiction or married her alcoholic husband). Angela started rejecting the heartfelt lie that somehow she needed to keep suffering for all the wrong she had done. In rejecting the lie, she slowly began to love—or at least like—herself. "I'm working on getting to the love part," she said.

However far she grows into self-compassion, Angela has already won very valuable ground in her recovery.

• • •

At an open AA meeting, Martha told of how she had smuggled bottles of liquor into an Arab country by hiding them in her infant daughter Kristen's stroller. Her husband had gotten a dream job in that faraway country and was not yet aware of the addiction his wife was bringing along with her. Smuggling alcohol into this country was a capital offense. In her addiction, Martha thought nothing of putting her daughter at such great risk.

That was sixteen years ago. Martha has now been clean and sober more than ten years. She said that her biggest obstacle in recovery was forgiving herself. What a terrible mother she had been. Didn't it follow that if she was a horrible mother, she was also a horrible person? And what right did a horrible person have to the gift of recovery? Even though she somehow stayed sober in those early years, she was miserable and full of self-loathing.

Years later, it was this same daughter who came to her rescue. Kristen had found Alateen. She had learned the principles of recovery—including self-forgiveness. One evening, Kristen confronted her mother. She told her to stop with the martyr act. She said she was tired of hearing her mother moaning about what she had done and what a horrible mother she was. The daughter told her mom that she couldn't change the past—but if she didn't get over this "pain-in-the-butt character defect," she was bringing the past with her right into the present. Kristen added, "That hurts me. Besides," she went on, "I'm fine. I love you, Mom. I want you to be happy and not always punishing yourself for what didn't happen."

Then the most amazing thing happened. At the meeting, Martha pointed out her daughter in the audience and asked the lovely young woman to stand up and be recognized. Martha publicly thanked her for her honesty and wisdom. Then she turned to the rest of us and said, "If any of you are refusing to forgive yourself—no matter what you've done or to whom you have done it—Kristen and I both encourage you to do the work, get over it, and stop being a 'pain in the butt' to everyone around you. Especially those who love you the most."

● ● ●

Is your spirit asking you for self-forgiveness? Maybe the time has come to

1. MAKE A DECISION that enough is enough! The program is not about beating yourself up. Nothing good comes from self-contempt.

2. UNDERSTAND AND OWN that refusing to forgive yourself is a character defect. As such, it blocks spirituality and joy in recovery.

3. EMBRACE whatever past situation is still causing you guilt and shame. (If it is not a past situation but a present one—STOP IT!) At long last, accept and emotionally embrace it. Don't run from it. Claim it as part of your life. The program cannot heal what we will not own.

4. SHARE with your vital connections (your Higher Power, self, and others) whatever it is you have owned and embraced. Hold it up so you're able to let it go—no matter what it is. A burden shared is cut in half. A burden not shared doubles in weight, shame, and guilt.

5. LIVE FREE of the enormous weight of refusing to forgive yourself. By far, the best way to make amends for whatever damage you've done in the past is to let it go and live free enough to help others learn to forgive themselves. Do you want to join the Great Endeavor? Forgiveness of self is the price of the ticket.

MAKE IT REAL

For many people, especially those programmed early in life toward self-contempt in any of its many forms, this very idea of forgiving self is about as tough as it gets. But it is even more necessary than it is tough. Recovery is about finding joy and refusing to be a "pain in the butt" to others, especially loved ones. That isn't possible for a person perpetually holding up a sign that says, "I AM BAD. PUNISH ME." So if this week's work touches a nerve, please do this work.

ACTION STEPS

Shame and regret can be crippling if we never say, "Enough is enough." If for no other reason, take care of this business for the sake of newcomers who will need your help. Holding a grudge against self is a crime against the future.

WRITE: (two or three paragraphs if you can, on the following topics. Give personal examples.)
1. If you still need self-forgiveness, describe the harm you've done to others by not forgiving yourself.
2. Explain why self-forgiveness is a critical element of your recovery.

SHARE: (with your group or sponsor)
1. Ask your group mates if and how your lack of self-forgiveness makes you a "pain in the butt."
2. Tell about something you're having trouble forgiving yourself for.

CONSCIOUS CONTACT: Pray for the ability to see yourself as your Higher Power sees you.

REACH OUT: Look around for another group mate who also struggles with self-forgiveness. Get together and discuss why refusing to forgive yourself is a "terrible waste of life."

• WEEK 51 •

Our Unconquered Spirit

Old-timers sometimes talk about the "two-steppers." Those are the folks who work only two Steps—the First and the Twelfth. After getting sober, they jump immediately to Twelfth-Stepping others. They skip all the work suggested by the Steps in between.

Not only do such people limit the power of what they have to give in their Twelve Step work, but they miss all the excitement and joy that comes from living a deeper spiritual life. They miss the thrill of experiencing "Yes, I can." They miss the wonder of grace that accompanies every promised spiritual awakening that comes through working the Steps. They miss the amazing transformative power of full participation in the Fellowship.

Against all odds—impossible odds, really—there are countless examples among us of those who have prevailed in recovery, have never given up, and have risen from the depths of despair to rewrite their stories in glory. Just as "there will come a time when no power on earth will keep you sober," it is also true that "God can and would if he were sought." And in that seeking and connection to the God of our understanding, there is no power anywhere, including addiction, that can capture and conquer a human spirit.

Like what? What glory? What connection? What victory against all odds? Here are a few stories of victory.

• • •

"My name is Rodney. Last week, I gave my sponsee his ninety-day chip at an awards meeting. The chip award before ours went to a woman named Sue. In her comments, she mentioned that she'd been a survivor of childhood sexual abuse. Her message was that with God's help, a person can survive anything.

"I certainly had not planned on sharing anything at this meeting except my congratulations to my sponsee. But I guess God had other plans. In the powerful way recovery sometimes picks you up and thrusts you on stage, I found myself at the front of the room holding the mike. I told them how Sue's comments had touched me—and then admitted that I had once been a sexual predator. I told them I wanted to express my sorrow for the harm I'd caused and to say that with God's grace and my hard work, I would never hurt anyone again.

"For several moments, no one moved or said a thing. Then Sue stood up and started to applaud. She led the way. Then one by one, everybody else stood up and applauded the victory of the spirit that recovery is for all of us."

• • •

"My name is Judy. I'm fifty-three years old and fifteen years sober. I guess I was as bad a drunk as ever existed. The bar in the little town where I did most of my drinking ran a pool on what day I would die. My skin was all yellow from my liver shutting down. My cholesterol was in the 600s. It got to where I was drinking in order to die. I *wanted* to die. Even as sick as I was, I realized that the way I was going, it was not worth staying alive.

"Somehow I got pregnant. I say 'somehow' because I have no idea who I was with or when it happened. It was a miracle I carried the baby to term. She lived three days. I have her face tattooed on my shoulder with wings wrapping around her. She's my little angel.

"My daughter's death slowed me down, but it didn't stop me. I know it was only grace that stopped my suicidal drinking—and that grace came through a man named Pat. At that time, I was getting a check from the county for $213 a month. To get it, though, I had to go to some classes on straightening out my life. You can imagine how I hated those classes! The woman who taught them was a bitch who constantly judged me and told me what a disgrace I was. So I quit the classes.

"Then a person I'd met called me up and told me to give the classes another try. She said they had a new teacher, a man named

Pat, who was an alcoholic like we were, only he was in recovery. I'll never forget the first time Pat looked at me. All these years later, it still makes me want to cry. *He looked at me like I was worth something.* He looked at me with love in his eyes—so I stayed. Pat and his wife stuck by me all the way through treatment and even after that.

"I don't know how those first steps work, but they do. I guess I must have been ready. But I know I wouldn't be sober today and sponsoring all the down-and-out women I do—women who were just like me—if Pat hadn't been there to love me. As long as I live, I'll be trying to help other suffering alcoholics to pay Pat back for being there for me."

• • •

Twenty years ago, Leo's son was going through treatment at the tender age of fourteen. At the time, Leo said his kid was a lazy, ungrateful, irresponsible idiot who deserved all the trouble he'd gotten into.

At one point during his son's treatment, Leo said he lost it completely. He really lit into his son, piling shameful, punishing words on top of the boy's head and heart. All these years later, Leo hung his head in shame at the memory.

The next day, he said, was family group. The counselor asked if any of the kids in the group ever felt like killing themselves. Leo thought the question was odd. Why would any of these kids feel like doing themselves in?

His son raised his hand and admitted he'd thought about ending it all. The counselor asked when this thought had come to him. The boy looked at his father and said, "Last night."

Leo said it felt like someone hit him in the teeth with a two-by-four. He said he'd never realized how much damage he was doing to his son, "whom I love with all my heart." Things were different from that moment on.

• • •

"My name is Julie. When I came into the program eight years ago, I never thought I would or could ever be 'spiritual.' I never thought for a moment that I'd ever have a 'spiritual experience' like some people in the program described. Not me. Not good old, alcoholic, dope addict Julie, who'd done it all, been kicked out of every place, stolen from my family, and woken up in bed with many men whose names

I didn't know and wouldn't want to remember. Spiritual experiences couldn't be for the likes of me. Maybe other people might have them, but not me. I figured I could never be 'one of them.'

"But I was wrong. I seriously underestimated the goodness and power of the God of my understanding. The ripples of God's grace never seem to run out of steam. Like last night at my Wednesday meeting.

"Some months ago, I'd been invited to participate in a Native American sweat ceremony. We were told that if it got too hot, we should lie on the ground next to Mother Earth, and she would cool us.

"Once in a while, the flap to the lodge would be opened to pass in a water bucket or because someone was leaving. The third and final time the flap opened, I could see through the steam that the only ones still sitting upright were the leader of the ceremony and myself. All the rest were lying on their Mother Earth.

"Something happened when I looked over at the leader. Instead of seeing *him,* I seemed to see an ancient Indian warrior chief. In my mind's eye, I can still see every piece of regalia he had on. He looked at me and said, 'You have power. Use it well.'

"Some people, I know, would say that I was hallucinating because of the extreme heat and loss of body fluid. But they can say anything they want. I know what I saw.

"Anyway, last night at the meeting, an older Native American gentleman named Larry got his seven-year pin. Larry has traveled such a rough road through life! Looking at him, you'd swear he didn't have fifteen minutes of sobriety, let alone seven years. But there he stood, a proud warrior.

"After the meeting, I went up to Larry. His eyes were cast down. (I'd been told that Native Americans consider it disrespectful to look into someone's eyes, especially a woman's.) I gave him a big hug anyway and congratulated him. He whispered soft as a breeze into my ear the most beautiful 'thank you' I've ever heard. When I started to walk away, he reached out for my hand. I took his hand and he looked into my eyes. I knew he was giving me a most precious gift. At that moment, the same ancient chief I had seen at the sweat ceremony flashed before my eyes. *I saw him in Larry.* Or maybe Larry was really that ancient warrior. I don't know, but I'll never forget that experience.

"I guess I am 'one of them' now."

MAKE IT REAL

The glory of your story is that you have survived addiction. And more than just survived, you've set about, with the help of those you stay connected with, to build your own house of spiritual values in recovery. Sometimes, in the busy blur of daily life, it's easy to lose sight of the glory. But to do so is like working all week and then neglecting to pick up your paycheck. In this case, your paycheck is the quality of life earned by working a deeply focused program. So what is the glory of *your* story?

ACTION STEPS

Call it by its name: There is real *glory* in moving from hopelessness to survival and on to a life of loving service. As long as we work the Steps in the context of the Fellowship, we have every reason to celebrate!

WRITE: (two or three paragraphs if you can, on the following topics. Give personal examples.)
1. Are you confident that your recovery is strong enough to endure? If not, explain why not.
2. What steps do you need to take to increase your confidence?

SHARE: (with your group or sponsor)
1. Tell your group mates about one or two new "chapters" you're aiming to add to your life story.
2. Tell about a mentor who's played a significant role in your recovery. What did that person do for you?

CONSCIOUS CONTACT: Humbly ask your Higher Power to enable you to envision your life "as it could be."

• • •

• **WEEK 52** •

Why Recovery Is Worth the Effort

So we come to the end—which is also just the beginning. In the introduction to this book, I mentioned that some people in our test group used this book by going back again and again to the specific week that most spoke to them. Or they used the material in a given week as the need arose in their lives. Of course, I recommended that everyone should gather a team of trusted others and work through all the weeks at least once. You never know what surprise might be waiting for you in a week you might just as easily have skipped over.

However you choose to use this book, it all comes back to deciding if the effort of committing to the program is worth it to you. Is it worth the effort to plow new ground, face old monsters, and start practicing a new way to live? It's all about "coming to believe" that *you* are worth the effort—and so are all the people you will be sent to help. Below are what a few others have said about why the effort of committing to the work of recovery and staying connected is worth it, at least for them. Why is it worth the effort to *you*?

• • •

Two men named James were at a dinner celebrating their first clean and sober year. Both had spent all their previous adult years "in the life." They had been street hustlers, drug dealers, "if you want it, take it" kind of guys. But now they were clean and sober and deep into a new way of life. Little James leaned over to James B. and in a voice laced with astonishment said, "Can you believe we're not living in fear? Can you *believe* we would ever live this life?" James B. said with equal astonishment, "No, man. Not in a thousand years. I always lived with a pistol under my mattress and another one under my pillow. I had motion detectors in my house and five attack dogs in my yard. Now I don't need any of that. I'm not afraid anymore because nobody can steal what counts to me now."

That's why it is worth it to them.

• • •

"My name is Abraham. I was a heroin addict for forty-six years. During that time, I spent twenty-five years in prison. There's not much in my life to be proud of. I've been clean and sober for a year now, and I'm so *proud* of that! Mostly what makes me proud is thinking of my mother, grandmother, and great-grandmother looking down at me from heaven. And I'll be clean and sober when I go to meet them."

That's why it is worth it to him.

• • •

"My name is Carl. In January 2000, I was eleven years sober. But nothing was going right for me. I was in constant mental and emotional pain, discouraged, and depressed. I felt like I didn't want to be in recovery anymore. The never-ending misery was just too much.

"The old-timers' words of advice weren't helping me. Then I heard about the word *codependent,* and I looked it up in the dictionary. I knew I needed to learn more. Even though I was in terrible shape, I picked up the phone and called one of the two places in Ontario, Canada, that had a family program dealing specifically with living problems.

"I had to wait until March for an opening. But after that week of learning about Al-Anon's principles and practices regarding life issues, everything fell into place. I didn't feel like the 'hole in the donut' anymore. Recovery began to make sense again, and the pain started to lift. I opened my ears, and pretty soon my heart opened also.

"It's been almost three years since then, and my recovery means *everything* to me now. My heart is healing in ways I never thought possible. It's like I've found new balance. For me, it takes *both* programs to find that 'joyful and free life' the Big Book promises."

That's why it is worth it to him.

• • •

"I'm Jack P., and I've been sober for almost six years. Recovery has made me so much more God-conscious. I love it. Have you heard the old saying that 'coincidence is God's way of staying anonymous'? I don't see it that way. I say coincidences are God's fingerprints on our lives. Like last week at our meeting, when a new man came in with two regulars. The new guy told an amazing story.

"With tears in his eyes, he said that he came to town for a convention but found himself in great need of a meeting. It sounded like he was pretty much in the same shape as Bill W. back in 1935 when he went to Akron and ended up at the Mayflower Hotel. He was right on the edge. So was this man.

"For some reason, he didn't think to call the AA hotline. He just took off walking down the street from his hotel. In a few minutes, our friend 'just happened' to pass the window of a coffee shop where our two regulars 'just happened' to be studying a Big Book before the meeting. The new guy 'just happened' to look in and recognize the blue and yellow cover that 'just happened' to be showing enough for him to see it.

"In he went to the coffee shop like a drowning man grabbing a wooden plank that 'just happened' to be floating by. He'd found members of his family 'totally by accident.' He was saved. They all went to a meeting.

"Go figure. I've been there. I guess if it had been me this time, I would have cried, too."

That's why it is worth it to him.

• • •

"Hi, everybody. I'm Helen. I've been clean and sober for twenty-two years. Just before I entered recovery, I had a baby son. I was in a bad way, and I knew I couldn't take care of him, so I gave him up for adoption. This year he'd be thirty years old. I've tried to find him, but haven't yet been able to. I work my program because if and when that blessed day comes, I want my son to find me sober."

That's why it is worth it to her.

• • •

"My name is Landon. I'm seventeen years sober. I grew up on what white people call an Indian reservation, but we call it home. When I was six years old, my father shot my mother to death and then killed himself because he thought she was cheating on him. Maybe she was. I don't know. I was so young when it happened, I don't really remember either of them very well.

"After my folks were gone, I was put in a Christian school. It was terrible. Every kind of abuse that could be put on a kid came to me. I think the worst was what I call 'culture abuse.' I was taught—all of us Indian kids were—that everything about our religion and rituals came from the devil. *They stole our culture from us.* And when you don't have a culture, you don't belong anywhere.

"I left the school and joined the Army when I was sixteen. The Army was better, even though it was there that I learned to drink and do drugs. My heart was so full of sadness and rage and emptiness that only alcohol and drugs gave me relief. I hated all white people and constantly thought of ways to get even for what had been done to me. The hate and the drugs were like a double-barreled shotgun that I aimed at my head every day.

"Then one night about fifteen years ago, I had a dream. For Indians, dreams are a two-way communication system with the spirit world. They're *real.* That night my grandmother came to me in this dream. She was the only person in my whole life I ever felt had loved me. In this dream, she held out her hand over me. A blue light coming from her hand shone over me. She told me that hate and the drugs I was using to kill my feelings were killing *me.* She told me to stop what I was doing and to listen. She told me I had the power to change my life if I would reconnect with the spirit world.

"At that moment, the hate and resentments vanished. They just weren't there anymore. I totally lost my interest in using again. Now it's all these years later, and I've committed my life to teaching the children about our culture and their place in the spirit world. I tell them the Creator who is our Grandfather will come to them, or send them someone who loves them, to show them the way to a spiritual life. If they ever get mixed up with drugs or alcohol, I tell them to not forget Grandfather because Grandfather never forgets them."

That's why it is worth it to him.

MAKE IT REAL

This is the last piece of work suggested in this book. It ends exactly where we started in Week 4—where you were asked to clarify what your addiction has cost you. In Week 52, I'm asking you to look at your life from the right side of the goalposts. What blessings have you gained from your recovery? Why is it worth any effort to foster and maintain those blessings? Do the work suggested, and then get up and dance on the kitchen table, or go out and bang pans in your front yard. Then fall on your knees and offer your heart's best prayer of thanksgiving for the gift of recovery that's so freely given to you.

ACTION STEPS

Attitude is everything. Is your glass half empty or half full? Positive or negative? Do you "have to" or "get to" do something about your life? *There is no substitute for an attitude of gratitude.*

WRITE: (two or three paragraphs if you can, on the following topics. Give personal examples.)
1. List two or three specific areas of your life that have improved since you got clean and sober.
2. How do you feel when you get up in the morning? Compare how you felt "then" and how you feel "now."

SHARE: (with your group or sponsor)
1. Describe the "gifts of recovery" you're most grateful for.

2. Share two realistic goals you're working toward that would have been impossible before recovery.

CONSCIOUS CONTACT: Ask your Higher Power for continuing willingness to focus on your gains.

REACH OUT: Look for upbeat, positive people in your group and arrange to spend time with them.

• • •

Close

There's a cavalcade of incredible recovering people, millions strong, passing your door. You'll never find a more thankful, joyful, and willing-to-help band of human beings than those in this group. They hold their hands out to you and invite you to join them—for the duration. If you're ever fearful or just plain tired or feeling especially lonely, let your heart and mind see this great cavalcade. *You are never alone.* You are never without resources, not as long as you choose to stay connected. All the help you will ever need is right there. Join them. Join me. Join us. We are all heading for the same place, high up the mountain. But the issue isn't how high we go, it's who we take with us, who our team is. So let's all go forth together, shoulder to shoulder, under the banner of *never give up*. That above all, my dear friends—NEVER, NEVER GIVE UP!

About the Authors

Earnie Larsen has been a grateful member of the Twelve Step family since 1966. In that time, he has written more than sixty recovery and spirituality books. He has authored dozens of DVDs and CD programs that have been a staple of recovery programs around the world for nearly thirty years. He is a much sought after speaker who has lectured extensively nationally and internationally. It has been said of him that, "His special gift seems to be ministering to the most broken among us." For more information on Larsen's programs, go to www.changeisachoice.com.

Starting out as a newspaper reporter, Carol Larsen Hegarty went on to educational publishing and worked as a program developer for several companies. She and her brother Earnie have collaborated on a number of books, including *Days of Joy, Believing in Myself,* and *Moving from Anger to Forgiveness.* She has been a grateful member of Al-Anon for thirty-eight years.